All in a Day's Work

Careers Using Science

2nd Edition

By Megan Sullivan for *The Science Teacher*

An NSTA Press Journals Collection

National Science Teachers Association

Arlington, Virginia

National Science Teachers Association

Claire Reinburg, Director
Jennifer Horak, Managing Editor
Judy Cusick, Senior Editor
Andrew Cocke, Associate Editor
Betty Smith, Associate Editor

Megan Sullivan, Managing Editor, *The Science Teacher*

ART AND DESIGN, Will Thomas, Jr., Art Director
Toni D. Jones, Graphic Designer

PRINTING AND PRODUCTION, Catherine Lorrain, Director
Nguyet Tran, Assistant Production Manager
Jack Parker, Electronic Prepress Technician

NATIONAL SCIENCE TEACHERS ASSOCIATION
Gerald F. Wheeler, Executive Director
David Beacom, Publisher

Library of Congress Cataloging-in-Publication Data

Sullivan, Megan (Megan M.)
All in a day's work : careers using science / by Megan Sullivan for the science teacher. — 2nd ed.
    p. cm.
Includes bibliographical references and index.
ISBN 978-1-93353-107-6
1. Science—Vocational guidance—United States. I. Title.
Q149.U5S92 2008
502.3—dc22
                    2008024672

NSTA is committed to publishing material that promotes the best in inquiry-based science education. However, conditions of actual use may vary, and the safety procedures and practices described in this book are intended to serve only as a guide. Additional precautionary measures may be required. NSTA and the authors do not warrant or represent that the procedures and practices in this book meet any safety code or standard of federal, state, or local regulations. NSTA and the authors disclaim any liability for personal injury or damage to property arising out of or relating to the use of this book, including any of the recommendations, instructions, or materials contained therein.

PERMISSIONS
You may photocopy, print, or e-mail up to five copies of an NSTA book chapter for personal use only; this does not include display or promotional use. Elementary, middle, and high school teachers *only* may reproduce a single NSTA book chapter for classroom- or noncommercial, professional-development use only. For permission to photocopy or use material electronically from this NSTA Press book, please contact the Copyright Clearance Center (CCC) (*www.copyright.com*; 978-750-8400). Please access *www.nsta.org/permissions* for further information about NSTA's rights and permissions policies.

CONTENTS

Introduction   vii
     By Steve Metz

Careers: Alphabetical List   xii

List of Academic Degrees   xiii

About the Author   xiv

CAREERS

Teacher
     Science teacher   2

The Adventurous Life
     Deep-cave explorer   6
     Firefighter and paramedic   8
     Astronaut   10

Animal Kingdom
     Arachnologist   14
     Animal nutritionist   16
     Aquaculture veterinarian   19
     Honey bee scientist   22
     Aquatic conservation biologist   25
     Oyster wrangler   28
     Shark advocate   31

Artistic Endeavors
     Scientific illustrator   36
     Art conservationist   38
     Landscape architect   40
     Musical acoustics scientist   42

Environmental Issues
     Environmental consultant   46
     Oceanographer   48
     Volcanologist   50
     Hurricane researcher   52
     Ethnobotanist   54

Health and Fitness

Diabetes educator   **58**
Genetic counselor   **60**
Radiation therapist   **62**
Respiratory therapist   **64**
Sport biomechanist   **67**
Ear, nose, and throat doctor   **70**
Clinical neuropsychologist   **73**

Let's Investigate

Cryptographer   **78**
Forensics services technician   **80**
Bomb investigator   **82**
Historical archaeologist   **84**
Dinosaur paleontologist   **87**
Bone detective   **89**

Research and Development

Industrial toxicologist   **94**
Coatings specialist   **96**
Microbiologist   **98**
Perfumer   **100**
Green product chemist   **103**
Cosmetic chemist   **105**

Technology—and Toys

Video game level designer   **108**
Automotive technician   **110**
Roller coaster designer   **112**
Artificial intelligence expert   **114**
Space architect   **116**
GIS specialist   **119**

What We Eat

NASA food scientist   **122**
Foodborne disease epidemiologist   **124**
Food technologist   **126**
Plant geneticist   **129**

References   **131**

Index   **133**

INTRODUCTION

All in a Day's Work, 2nd Edition—with 15 new careers—is aimed at giving high school students a taste of the diversity of careers in which science is used and at making them aware of how increasingly important science learning is in today's world. The book is a collection of case stories about people who use science every day in their careers. This compendium of columns from the NSTA journal *The Science Teacher* looks at the many careers for which science is necessary. They range from the expected—high school science teacher, microbiologist, and forensics technician—to the perhaps unexpected—firefighter, landscape architect, and historical archaeologist—to the adventurous—astronaut, deep-cave explorer, and oceanographer—and to the offbeat—roller coaster designer, perfumer, and sport biomechanist.

Budget cuts in high school guidance offices often make it difficult for students looking for information about careers. It is easy—and common—to drift through school science and math classes wondering, "Why do I need to learn this?" Many students do not see a college science major or science career in their future, making the need to learn science less than obvious. Of course, the best reason for learning science is that understanding science is important in and of itself, as part of humankind's search for knowledge and meaning. Understanding science makes everything—a walk in the woods, reading a newspaper or watching the news on TV, a family visit to a science museum or beach—more *interesting*. The grand enterprise that is science springs from the most basic and fundamental of human desires: to make sense of the world.

But the next-best answer to the question—why do I need to learn this?—may be more practical and persuasive. As the stories in *All in a Day's Work* show, learning science and mathematics can lead to meaningful, interesting life's work. The careers featured in this book provide a good sense of the vast array of science fields that will be available to those having the interest and preparation. They are divided into categories that hint at this wide diversity: adventure, mystery, animals, health, technology, and art. Information also is provided about related careers. Taken together, the case stories provide essential perspectives on the many ways science learning is increasingly important in today's world of jobs and careers.

Photocopies of many of the stories found in *All in a Day's Work* have found their way into high school guidance offices and onto science classroom bulletin boards. They give a fascinating glimpse of what it is like to *do* science from people actually engaged in applying science in their daily work lives. The stories are interesting in and of themselves, but they also give practical information about educational and other career requirements.

Each of the people profiled here gives specific, no-nonsense insider's advice for those interested in pursuing the career, including where to go for additional information. Maybe even more important, reading these stories may trigger hidden interests. Gee, I didn't know I could do *that!* Or, Wow, what a cool job—I'd like to do *that!* As foodborne disease scientist Jack Guzewich observes (p. 124), "I had no idea such a career even existed when I was in high school or college." Perhaps reading *All in a Day's Work* will spare you a similar experience. Each of the 49 stories in this book is unique, and the advice about education and training is tightly focused to the particular requirements of each career. Still, common themes appear over and over:

The only thing certain is that nothing is certain. In these stories you will hear about the often-winding paths that take a person to a given career. Futurists predict that individuals will have many careers—and numerous jobs within each field—over the course of a life span. More than ever before, students today need to plan for different work roles and opportunities. Even people who share a common career usually come to it from varied backgrounds. *All in a Day's Work* contains stories of a hopeful Olympic gymnast who is now a sport biomechanist, a would-be accountant turned respiratory therapist, a music major now working as a video game designer, an aspiring science teacher who found a career as a food scientist, a roller coaster designer who originally planned to become an architect, and many other tales of false starts and changing careers. These stories demonstrate how rarely the path to a single career is straightforward, giving hope to those struggling to discover what they want to do in life. Most career paths are neither straight nor predictable—and who would want them to be? Careers can have as many sudden turns as life itself—it's one of the things that makes life interesting.

Education is more important than ever. The advice from these interviews appears loud and clear: Stay in school, study hard, take as much science and math as possible. Still, not every science career requires years and years of schooling or multiple advanced degrees. In fact, job growth for specialized PhDs will probably be flatter than for those with broader, more multidisciplinary training. Some of the careers in *All in a Day's Work* require extensive advanced academic study, while others offer positions for those with a high school diploma. They all require a foundation of education and training that begins in high school or even earlier. *Learning is lifelong.* After you accept that nothing is certain and education is more important than ever, it naturally follows that learning must be continued throughout life. Virtually every career in *All in a Day's Work*—from auto technician to artificial intelligence expert, bomb investigator, genetic counselor, and all the rest—requires lifelong learning.

There are many paths to discovering what you want to do and what you will become. All in a Day's Work profiles people who were inspired by high school teachers, parents, summer jobs and internships, after-school programs, and personal hobbies. Hurricane researcher Christopher Landsea became interested in meteorology though a community research program at his high school and also a love of windsurfing. Perfumer Christophe Laudamiel was inspired at a young age by the fragrances from his family's kitchen and gardens. As he was growing up, oceanographer Evan Forde always loved water sports and was inspired by a television show, *The Undersea World of Jacques Cousteau.* Arachnologist Paula Cushing became interested in spiders while in high school, through volunteer work as a park naturalist and a summer internship at the Smithsonian Institution. As these and other case stories demonstrate, there are many routes to a career that uses science. Visiting museums, watching documentaries, reading, and gaining work experience through summer jobs, volunteer work, or internships can all provide valuable guidance and direction. Paying attention in science and math classes can help, too!

Most careers require multidisciplinary approaches. Specialized scientists will always play an important role, but the case stories in *All in a Day's Work* show that cross-discipline problem solving is essential in a wide variety of careers. Auto mechanics apply chemistry and physics concepts; oceanographers require preparation in biology, geology, and other physical sciences; scientific illustrators need a good background in all the science disciplines. Art conservationist Susan Barger credits her success to a college double major in art and French and an interdisciplinary doctorate in materials science, chemistry, and the history of technology. A solid grounding in all the basic sciences is a good start for any career. Interpersonal skills and teamwork, as well as communication and critical-thinking abilities, can prove invaluable. These skills can be developed over time through inquiry-based science investigations and cooperative classroom activities.

Almost all careers in the 21st century require a working knowledge of science and mathematics. The case stories in this book only scratch the surface of the many careers open to those who have a science background. The increasingly technological nature of modern society places a premium on those with science and math training. From 1980 to 2000 the number of science and engineering careers increased more than four times the rate of growth for all jobs, and expansion of S & E occupations is predicted to continue to remain higher than for the labor force as a whole (Science and Engineering Indicators 2004). It is difficult to imagine a future career for which a science background would not be at least helpful, if not truly essential. The pending retirement of 78 million baby boomers can only add to the need for science and mathematics training, as companies begin recruiting replacement workers in science fields, sometimes—believe it or not—as early as *middle school!*

Science is for all. While barriers still exist, science careers are opening up to underrepresented groups as never before. The story of NASA astronaut Ellen Ochoa is hopeful. In her case story she notes that women weren't accepted into the astronaut corps until she was halfway through college. Her science education ultimately allowed her to become the first Hispanic woman to fly on a mission to space—she now is a veteran of four missions—and to perform science and technology experiments aboard the Space Shuttle and International Space Station. In 2000 women earned between 40% and 60% of the bachelor's degrees awarded in mathematics and in physical, Earth, ocean, and atmospheric sciences. Their share of engineering degrees has increased dramatically from the mid-1970s to the present. Also during the same period, the percentage of nonwhite students earning science bachelor's degrees more than doubled (Science and Engineering Indicators 2004). The case studies in *All in a Day's Work* illustrate the wide diversity of people who are drawn to science careers.

Science is creative. The persistent image of the clipboard-holding scientist in a white lab coat does much to foster the illusion that science is dull, dry, and uncreative. Nothing could be further from the truth. Pure science is among humankind's most creative endeavors, and science is applied in a wide range of interesting, creative fields. As the case stories in *All in a Day's Work* show, science careers offer a place for art conservationists and illustrators, music majors and architects, perfumers and landscape designers, video game creators and cryptographers. Creativity is virtually a prerequisite for most science-related careers.

Science careers are among the most interesting and rewarding. The scientists of *All in a Day's Work* often are asked to describe a typical day at work, and animal nutritionist Mark

X

Edwards's response is shared by most: "There really isn't a typical day at work—an aspect of my job that I particularly enjoy." Science-related careers like those described in this book require tackling new challenges and solving interesting problems on a daily basis.

Chance favors the prepared mind (Louis Pasteur). In its own way, each of the stories in *All in a Day's Work* points out the importance of being ready for opportunities that often arise from chance events and encounters. A family illness led Robert Adams to a career in radiation therapy. Respiratory therapist John Hiser credits being drafted into the Navy during the Vietnam War for his ultimate career choice. Others in this book have similar stories to tell. The constant theme in these vignettes is that solid preparation in background science knowledge consistently opens doors to many career opportunities.

You can do it. Career counseling can be difficult to obtain as budget cuts force schools to reduce their guidance departments. The good news is that information about science-related careers has never been easier to find. The case stories in *All in a Day's Work* include suggestions about how to find additional career information, including links to the websites of relevant professional organizations and interest groups. So read the personal stories in *All in a Day's Work*, find ones that interest you, and go check out the recommended internet sites for more information. Even better, find someone in your area working in a particular career that you think might be interesting. Like the men and women interviewed for this book, most professionals love to showcase and discuss their careers with young people.

The advice found in this book is as ancient as Confucius: "Find a job that you love, and you will never have to work a day in your life." The people profiled here have found jobs that they love. Their careers are interesting, often exciting, and in ways small and large they help make the world a better place. And who knows? Reading about them might just inspire you to join their ranks.

Steve Metz
Field Editor
The Science Teacher

Reference
Science and Engineering Indicators 2004 (National Science Board). Accessed July 31, 2006. *www.nsf.gov/statistics/seind04*

CAREERS

Alphabetical List

Animal nutritionist	16	GIS specialist	119
Aquaculture veterinarian	19	Green product chemist	103
Aquatic conservation biologist	25	Historical archaeologist	84
Arachnologist	14	Honey Bee scientist	22
Art conservationist	38	Hurricane researcher	52
Artificial intelligence expert	114	Industrial toxicologist	94
Astronaut	10	Landscape architect	40
Automotive technician	110	Microbiologist	98
Bomb investigator	82	Musical acoustics scientist	42
Bone detective	89	NASA food scientist	122
Clinical neuropsychologist	73	Oceanographer	48
Coatings specialist	96	Oyster wrangler	28
Cosmetic chemist	105	Perfumer	100
Cryptographer	78	Plant geneticist	129
Deep-cave explorer	6	Radiation therapist	62
Diabetes educator	58	Respiratory therapist	64
Dinosaur paleontologist	87	Roller coaster designer	112
Ear, nose, and throat doctor	70	Science teacher	2
Environmental consultant	46	Scientific illustrator	36
Ethnobotanist	54	Shark advocate	31
Firefighter and paramedic	8	Space architect	116
Foodborne disease epidemiologist	124	Sport biomechanist	67
Food technologist	126	Video game level designer	108
Forensics services technician	80	Volcanologist	50
Genetic counselor	60		

ACADEMIC DEGREES

These are some of the degrees that people in this book have earned.

AA—associate of arts

BA—bachelor of arts

BFA—bachelor of fine arts

BS—bachelor of science

DVM—doctor of veterinary medicine

EdD—doctor of education

MAA—master of applied anthropology

MEd—master of education

MFA—master of fine arts

MPH—master of public health

MS—master of science

PhD—doctor of philosophy

VMD—see DVM

ABOUT THE AUTHOR

Megan Sullivan is the managing editor of *The Science Teacher* and a member of the National Association of Science Writers. Her background includes a BS in integrated science and technology and an honors education from James Madison University. She has conducted research in a National Aeronautics and Space Administration lab, mountaineered in the High Sierras, and lived in Italy. She is also a yoga teacher and a freelance writer/editor.

TEACHER

Teacher

SCIENCE TEACHER

If you are interested in science and have a gift for explaining it to others, you might want to consider a future in science teaching. You don't have to go far to learn more about this career niche: A wealth of information may literally be staring you in the face. Who are your science teachers? What are their backgrounds? Ask questions, and you'll learn that there's more than meets the eye. From challenging eager learners to encouraging those who think they can't do science, high school science teacher Mike Zito says there's nothing like seeing the lights go on in students' minds. To him, the best part of teaching is crafting and executing a rich lesson plan that brings students to a true understanding of science.

DESCRIBE A TYPICAL DAY.

Teaching is a wonderful combination of science and interpersonal interactions. The best part of the job is inspiring young minds by sharing my joy and wonder for science. The time in front of the classroom is the easiest and most fun part of the day, but a good lesson requires meticulous preparation. A typical day begins with arriving early and making sure the classroom is prepared for the day's activities. Science teaching differs from teaching many other disciplines due to the extra effort involved in preparing a laboratory-intensive experience for students. I spend the afternoon in any number of ways: evaluating student work, cleaning the lab of the day's activity, attending faculty meetings, meeting with parents and students, or sponsoring clubs. Back at home, some of the evening is spent grading or planning what I hope will be interesting lessons for the next unit.

WHAT BACKGROUND IS NEEDED?

A bachelor's degree in a scientific field is absolutely necessary, and a master's degree in science is a great plus. In addition, teachers must take courses in education and child development as required by their particular state to receive a teaching license. Continuing education in both scientific and educational disciplines is needed to maintain licensure during a teaching career. Laboratory experience in an academic or industrial setting is an asset that brings a real-world perspective to your teaching.

As an undergraduate, I majored in biology and minored in chemistry. After college, I worked for five years in the field of genetic toxicology while attending night school to get a master's in environmental science. I went on to receive my teaching certification. My continuing education courses include graduate courses in environmental

2

modeling and analysis, understanding by design, and teacher expectations and student achievement.

ANY ADVICE FOR STUDENTS?

The unique aspect of this career is that students can observe a great deal of a science teacher's daily work. Students interested in science teaching must actively seek to gain a greater appreciation for the less visible aspects of the job. They should spend some time on the other side of the desk. They should get to know their teachers as people, talk with teachers about their careers, and offer to help set up and tear down labs. Students can also volunteer to tutor other science students and read professional journals.

HOW DID YOU CHOOSE TEACHING?

I sort of fell into teaching, I didn't really set out to be a teacher. My choice of a college major was more to satisfy my intellectual curiosity and love of science than it was to prepare for a career. I have always been a science geek. As a child, my favorite toys were microscopes and chemistry sets. Outside,

Mike Zito likes sharing the "joy and wonder for science" with his students.

I could be found down at the local pond catching frogs and watching the wildlife. I always wanted to know why and how—science offered those answers. As my own sense of wonder and delight about science grew, I began to share those insights with others. When I worked as a laboratory teaching assistant in graduate school, I found I had a knack for explaining science to others and that I enjoyed working with young people. I soon quit my job in genetic toxicology and went to school full time to get my teaching certificate. I have never looked back.

	EDUCATION	ON THE WEB	RELATED CAREERS
BONUS POINTS	BS, biology, minor in chemistry; MS, environmental science	National Science Teachers Association (*www.nsta.org*)	museum educator, science outreach coordinator, scientific illustrator, science writer, broadcast science journalist, college biology professor, science curriculum coordinator

THE ADVENTUROUS LIFE

The Adventurous Life

DEEP-CAVE EXPLORER

Barbara Anne am Ende first learned about the wonders of caving during a visit to a commercial cave at the age of 14. Shortly thereafter she took a spelunking tour—studying caves and their contents—and was hooked. She joined the National Speleological Society (NSS) to foster her interest. As a member, she did some tourist caving, looking around well-known systems and visiting wild caves, which are undeveloped and without paths or lights. Am Ende longed to find a passage no person had ever seen before, a virgin cave. She got her wish: One of her most memorable explorations, the 1994 Huautla Expedition, is depicted in her book, *Beyond the Deep*.

WHAT DOES A DEEP-CAVE EXPLORER DO?

Most hard-core cavers live to scoop booty—to be the first person ever in a cave. Some cavers aspire to set depth records, and others find a system to keep exploring until they have seen it all. However, it's not enough to just see a cave. The passage has to be mapped. Cavers suit up in nylon coveralls, helmets with efficient lamps, and sturdy boots. Survey equipment traditionally is composed of a compass, clinometer [used to measure angles], and fiberglass tape. A typical team may include a lead who heads first into the unknown with one end of the survey tape, a second person to hold the tape's other end, and a third party to document distances, angles, and cave sketches. With this data, the survey line is later plotted on a computer. More recently, I have used survey equipment that maps caves in 3-D. The device sends laser [or sonar, if underwater] beams out within the cave and records reflections from the walls. Complex software converts those measurements into a virtual cave. Someday we will be able to go caving without setting foot underground, which will be useful for educational outreach and scientific studies.

Because cave exploration is not a well-paid profession, I choose to also have a day job with the Aerospace Corporation, where I combine geology and computer skills to study the Earth through remote sensing. As part of The Matrix, I get farmed out to various projects that need someone with my expertise. I am constantly learning new things, the job never gets boring, and my caving career remains a special treat.

WHAT BACKGROUND IS NEEDED?

The caving community includes a lot of different backgrounds. Within caves, geologists may study mineralogy, hydrologists investigate water movement, and microbiologists can examine bacteria. Engineers design equipment used in cave exploration and research. Archaeologists study cave paintings and artifacts to learn about past cultures. Sketch artists and photographers detail cave walls and features. Rescue work is yet another aspect of caving.

Students should visit the NSS website at *www.caves. org* to find links to grottoes—local caving clubs that organize trips and provide proper caving equipment and important safety guidelines for members.

WHAT HAS BEEN YOUR MOST EXCITING EXPERIENCE?

The 1994 Huautla Expedition, in Mexico, involved one of the deepest caves in the Americas at the time. My team sought to explore and map this cave in hopes it would prove to be the deepest in the world. The route we took into the cave descended about 840 m before we hit a point that was completely

Barbara Anne am Ende held a depth record in caving from 1994 to 2003.

flooded with water, an obstacle we intended to beat. At that depth, we camped on a collapsible platform and started to dive through the water with rebreathers [a type of scuba gear that recirculates a diver's breath instead of losing the exhalation as bubbles]. It was a very difficult project, and most of our team quit during the three months on site. In the end, only the expedition leader and I dove through the flooded section of the cave to emerge into air and explore another 3 km stretch of virgin cave. That set the depth record for caves in all the Americas at −1475 m, a record that lasted for nine years and was broken by only a scant 9 m in 2003.

BONUS POINTS	EDUCATION BS, MS, PhD, geology	ON THE WEB National Speleological Society (*www.caves.org*)	RELATED CAREERS oceanographer, marine biologist, hydrogeologist, archaeologist, underwater photojournalist, technical diver, wreck diver, polar explorer

The Adventurous Life

FIREFIGHTER AND PARAMEDIC

Denise Dierich has forged a unique career path from biochemistry and teaching to firefighting and paramedics. Her appreciation for science constantly yields new challenges and rewards as she provides a vital service to her community. One of the aspects Dierich likes best about her job is that, like science, it is dynamic and there are always new things to learn.

WHAT INSPIRED YOUR CAREER ENDEAVORS?

Growing up in Alaska, I appreciated the value of understanding the biological world. Later, in high school, a biology teacher extended this interest through various field trips and lab demonstrations—science became more than just words in a book. As an undergraduate, I was drawn to biochemistry because it offered explanations of natural phenomena and how organisms work. Although the science itself was fascinating, I found the lab work to be tedious, so I pursued a career in science education, which was anything but boring. Just as teaching is service oriented, so is being a firefighter. I left teaching to become a firefighter because it also incorporates many of my ambitions and interests and provides the opportunity to help people and communities. As I worked on aid calls [when a fire engine accompanies a paramedic unit],

I realized I could apply my science background and enthusiasm for learning by becoming a paramedic.

DESCRIBE A TYPICAL DAY.

We work 24-hour shifts. The day starts with an informal report from the previous crew involving issues with equipment and potential problems. Rig checks [fuel, fluids, equipment, gear, and lights] are performed to ensure the apparatus is in proper working order. Next, our captain assigns training and duties for the day, which consist, for example, of hose evolutions, emergency medical technician practice scenarios, pump operation, and hydraulic system exercises. Continual training is essential. Because the job is so multifaceted, skills and knowledge must be constantly reinforced. Training may be interrupted if there is a call, which could be a medical or fire emergency, a motor vehicle accident, a fire alarm, a hazardous spill, or a public

8

assist request. We respond to a variety of situations. Each day, and every call, is different.

HOW DO YOU USE SCIENCE?

The problem-solving skills developed through my science education have been very beneficial. Because no fire or aid call is the same, we have to constantly evaluate situations and react appropriately. My background in biochemistry and study skills acquired through college science classes have been instrumental in preparing for the academic portion of the paramedic program—a commitment that involves several courses and certification tests.

"Continual training is essential," says Denise Dierich.

ADVICE FOR STUDENTS?

The more education obtained, the better. The only specific requirement is a high school diploma. A bachelor's degree, however, shows self-discipline and the ability to complete tasks. Firefighting has become a very popular and competitive field—600 people tested for five openings in our last round. For some areas of advancement, a bachelor's degree is required. Also, most firefighting tests include a fitness component, which can be quite demanding.

Investigate the possibilities for a ride-along with local fire departments. Many firefighters and paramedics allow civilians to ride a medic unit or engine for part of a day. Consider joining a volunteer fire department; they will provide training and valuable experience. Some volunteer districts even provide housing at the station and help finance college tuitions.

BONUS POINTS	EDUCATION	ON THE WEB	RELATED CAREERS
	BS, biochemistry; secondary teaching credential, biology and chemistry; emergency medical technician (EMT) paramedic certification	National Association of Emergency Medical Technicians (*www. naemt.org*); International Association of Fire Fighters (*www.iaff.org*)	police officer, detective, air traffic controller, registered nurse, physician's assistant

The Adventurous Life

ASTRONAUT

If there is no career exciting enough for you here on Earth, then shoot for the stars—literally. Space is less of a mystery than it used to be, thanks in no small part to the courageous men and women who travel to the outer stretches of our universe. NASA astronaut Ellen Ochoa, the first Hispanic woman to fly on a mission to space, loves being a part of something much bigger than herself—humankind's endeavor to journey throughout our vast universe and understand what it's like to live in space. When Ochoa performs science and technology experiments on the space missions of today, she also sets the stage for the explorations of tomorrow.

HOW DID YOU BECOME AN ASTRONAUT?

Having grown up during the Apollo era, I avidly followed flights to the Moon along with everyone else. However, women were not accepted into the astronaut corps until I was halfway through college, so I had not considered it as a career when I was young. The first shuttle flight lifted off when I was a graduate student at Stanford University, and a couple of years later NASA was accepting applications for another astronaut class. I was doing research at the time, so I was especially intrigued with the idea of doing research in the unique space environment, along with the thrill of space flight. I was very excited to learn that I would be eligible to apply as soon as I finished my doctorate, and that is exactly what I did.

I am fortunate to carry out a very exciting, visible role, which has included running experiments in space, operating robot arms to deploy satellites, installing modules onto the International Space Station, and assisting the commander and pilot in launch, rendezvous, and landing procedures. But I do not work alone. I am part of a team that includes not only the crew but also the entire team of people who make a mission successful. Everyone works very hard to do their parts in planning, designing, and executing a mission, and each person's job is important.

DESCRIBE WHAT YOU DO.

One aspect of my job that I really enjoy is the variety. When I am training for a flight, I spend a lot of time in simulators planning, rehearsing, and problem solving for all phases of a mission.

Astronaut Ellen Ochoa is the first Hispanic woman to fly on a space mission.

For example, we use a motion-based simulator to practice launches and landings, robotic simulators—both computer-based and hardware-based, including one underwater—to practice the tasks involving robot arms, and experimental hardware or software to learn about scientific procedures. One day I might fly in a high-performance jet to Florida to train with some hardware there and gain crew coordination experience. Another day I might scuba dive in our big training pool to learn about the tasks being performed by the spacewalking crewmembers on my flight.

When not in training, I have held many interesting positions that support the shuttle and station programs. I have helped develop updated robotic procedures, tested out flight software, worked in Mission Control as the liaison between the on-orbit crew and the control team, and led the Astronaut Office support to the Space Station Program, which included negotiations with members of the Russian Space Agency. I am currently in a management position as deputy director of the organization that includes the Astronaut Office and aircraft operations that support astronaut training. My boss and I represent the crew at major technical and mission meetings as well as manage the policy, budget, and personnel for our organization.

ANY ADVICE FOR STUDENTS?

Astronauts must have a college degree in a technical field—some area of science, engineering, math, or medicine. Most astronauts have at least a master's degree, and many mission specialists, like me, have either a doctorate or medical degree. My bachelor's degree is in physics, and my master's degree and doctorate are in electrical engineering with a specialization in optical information processing.

My science education has enabled me to learn every necessary detail of the shuttle systems. I need to understand how the propulsion, electrical power, mechanical, life support, flight control, and communications systems all work—well enough to diagnose, troubleshoot, and recover from problems. We have support from all the folks on the ground, but we must always be prepared for a situation in which communications with the ground team are lost. The specific research that I did in optics, prior to becoming an astronaut, came in most handy on my first two flights. We carried out a number of experiments that studied the ozone hole and the effect of the Sun's radiation on the creation and destruction of ozone—many of these were optics-based experiments that I needed to understand as well as describe to the general public before, during, and after my flight.

Students can check out NASA's website about astronauts at *http://astronauts.nasa.gov* and also read astronauts' first-hand experiences at *www.nasa.gov/centers/johnson/about/people/astronotes.html*.

AN EXPERIENCE THAT STANDS OUT TO YOU?

It is hard to pick just one experience because I have had so many amazing ones since joining the astronaut corps. All four of my spaceflights have been unforgettable. I vividly recall seeing Earth for the first time, trying to get used to moving around and working in zero gravity—it takes both less physical effort and more mental concentration than one might think—and the thrill of working with my crew to accomplish a difficult task, such as installing a 12 m truss structure on the International Space Station.

I have a lingering memory from my last flight. The Sun set shortly after we undocked from the Space Station and as we moved away we could see just a shadow of the station, illuminated by the lights of the shuttle. The limb of Earth was behind the station, and, as we neared the most southern part of our orbit, we witnessed the southern lights. Ghostly green filaments stretched tens if not hundreds of kilometers into space in ever-changing patterns, with some red bursts of color at the tips. This beautiful, eerie sight mesmerized the crew. Suddenly it was sunrise, and the whole station turned a brilliant white and gold as if a cloaking device had just been removed. It was an incredible moment not just because of what we saw but also because of whom we saw it with. Working so closely with a team to accomplish a challenging, meaningful task is the greatest reward of being an astronaut.

BONUS POINTS	EDUCATION BS, physics; MS, PhD, electrical engineering	ON THE WEB NASA Astronaut Selection *(http://astronauts.nasa.gov)*; NASA Johnson Space Center astronaut profiles and experiences *(www.nasa.gov/centers/johnson/about/people/astronotes.html)*	RELATED CAREERS astronomer, physicist, nuclear engineer, pilot, audiovisual specialist, meteorologist

12

ANIMAL KINGDOM

Animal Kingdom

ARACHNOLOGIST

Do you find scorpions fascinating, daddy longlegs elegant, and think that spiders get a bad rap? If so, you may be suited for a career as an arachnologist—a scientist who studies the biology of these animals. As an arachnologist, Paula E. Cushing's proudest accomplishment is leading a team to update and revise *Spiders of North America: An Identification Manual*. Cushing is also a curator of invertebrate zoology at the Denver Museum of Nature & Science, which allows her to share her passion with scientists, teachers, students, artists, and the rest of us.

WHAT IS ARACHNOLOGY?

Arachnids consist of more than 90,000 discovered species, including spiders, scorpions, daddy longlegs, camel spiders [or solifugids], ticks, and mites. Arachnologists study some aspect of the biology of one or more of these groups of animals, and the field is called arachnology. For example, I study the evolutionary relationships among different species of camel spiders in the order Solifugae. I also study the evolutionary ecology of tiny spiders that live symbiotically inside the nest chambers of an ant species. In addition, I conduct a biodiversity project—the Colorado Spider Survey *(www.dmns.org/spiders/default.aspx)*—surveying and documenting the different species of spiders found in the Rocky Mountain ecoregion.

HOW DID YOU BECOME AN ARACHNOLOGIST?

I have had an interest in science and in the natural world since childhood. In high school I knew I wanted to be a biologist and a researcher, so throughout my teens I volunteered as a naturalist at a local park. One summer, I interned in the Insect Zoo at the Smithsonian Institution's National Museum of Natural History in Washington, DC, and started learning about the natural history of insects and spiders. My freshman year of

Paula Cushing became interested in spiders at the Smithsonian Institution's Insect Zoo.

college, I was interested in researching the biology of arthropods and volunteered in a biology professor's laboratory. He was an arachnologist and he became my mentor, taught me about spiders and research, and took me to my first scientific conference to present a project he and I worked on together. The field of arachnology has only about 1,000 researchers worldwide, and the other scientists at the meeting were very supportive of student research. I was not only fascinated with the organisms, but I was also attracted to the collegial and supportive atmosphere I found at that first meeting.

DESCRIBE YOUR JOB.

For science in any field to progress, scientists must collaborate and support one another, and must be willing to translate their passion and knowledge to the general public. This is where my job comes in. As a curator, I combine research and outreach to bridge the gap between scientists and the public. The research aspect involves conducting scientific studies and overseeing collections of preserved invertebrates—arachnids, insects, and shells. Data associated with these specimens tell scientists where the organisms were collected, when

they were collected, and who collected them. Thus, studying these museum specimens can inform us about the biodiversity of the different habitats of Earth and can indicate how this biodiversity has changed over time. The outreach side entails teaching, lecturing, attending workshops, conducting behind-the-scenes tours, and staying involved with professional scientific societies in my field.

ANY ADVICE FOR STUDENTS?

The best way for students to learn about spiders and other arachnids is to observe them. Students should find out if local parks and natural areas need volunteer naturalists. Internships are available through some museums and zoos. Local university professors or museum curators may need help in the laboratory. Students who have a serious interest in science should never be afraid to e-mail or contact a scientist for advice. Students should be formal, polite, and, most important, prepared with organized and clear questions. They can obtain a wealth of information just by interviewing a scientist or sending a researcher a list of thoughtful questions.

BONUS POINTS	EDUCATION BS, biology; MS, zoology; PhD, zoology	ON THE WEB American Arachnological Society (www. americanarachnology. org); International Society of Arachnology (www. arachnology.org); American Tarantula Society (http:// atshq.org)	RELATED CAREERS entomologist, zoologist, biology lab technician, high school biology teacher

ANIMAL NUTRITIONIST

As an animal nutritionist with the Zoological Society of San Diego, Mark Edwards loves being part of a program that provides world-class, science-based care for animals. The experience he brings to his job—he previously worked as an animal keeper, wildlife rehabilitator, field biologist, and laboratory technician—helps Edwards meet his main objective, which is to ensure that the zoo inhabitants thrive in their environment.

WHAT INSPIRED YOU TO BECOME AN ANIMAL NUTRITIONIST?

While growing up on a small suburban farm in Cincinnati, I was fascinated with animal care and diets. I looked after everything from raccoons and opossums to pygmy goats, sheep, and llamas. My parents nurtured my curiosity by taking me on regular trips to the local zoo, natural history museum, and nature centers.

In high school, my studies were heavily biased toward sciences—I knew I wanted to work in a zoo, but I did not completely understand what that encompassed. I began volunteering at the Cincinnati Zoo as soon as I got my driver's license, which gave me great exposure to the types of jobs available in the field.

I went on to pursue a bachelor's degree in zoology. During my fourth year as an undergraduate, I was selected for an internship at the Smithsonian Institution's National Zoo. As an intern, I cared for red pandas who were being studied for a nutritional needs project. The people involved in the project inspired me to pursue a career in animal nutrition. I now have a doctorate in animal science with a comparative animal nutrition emphasis.

WHAT DOES AN ANIMAL NUTRITIONIST DO?

Zoo nutritionists supervise the daily administration of animals, which includes managing the people, facilities, and budgets needed to support these operations. As a subject matter expert, I work closely with the keeper, curatorial, and veterinary staff to ensure that all animals receive healthy, nutritionally balanced meals. I am responsible for formulating many of the foods prepared for the animals. Consequently, I also work with the animal care staff to objectively evaluate an animal's response to a particular diet or feeding program [based on an animal's weight, body condition, and fecal consistency, for example].

There really is not a typical day at work—an aspect of my job that I particularly enjoy. I might be found at the San Diego Zoo's Wild Animal Park, starting the day early with a walk around the hospital. Or, along with the animal care staff, I might review cases for patients currently in the hospital and then prioritize the day's schedule. For instance, if a Bornean Sunbear is sedated for a physical exam, we collect body measurements, which can be used to develop species-specific tools that evaluate the bear's condition.

Another part of the job includes working with suppliers to make sure the animals' foods are wholesome and safe—stored, processed, and prepared to maintain nutritional quality. Quality control samples of all foods are collected routinely for chemical analysis, submitted to laboratories, and reviewed. Also, there are often several special ongoing projects, including working with field biologists in the research division. I am currently assisting with a project studying the impact of nutrition on desert bighorn sheep habitat selection, and another project evaluating habitat and food sources for iguanas in the Caribbean.

WHAT BACKGROUND IS NEEDED?

The diversity of topics and critical thinking needed to provide nutrition support for zoo animals

Mark Edwards improved the health of pandas.

typically demands a doctorate-level degree in the science of nutrition. Because the field is still very young, a standard degree has not been defined; a degree in veterinary medicine followed with a master's degree in nutrition would prepare an individual to pursue a career in animal nutrition. The most important skills needed are adaptability and objectivity. Even if a position or project requires working with only a small portion of an animal's physiology, it helps to understand and appreciate the whole animal—learn about its biology, the habitat where it is found, and how the work contributes to its conservation.

It is important to keep in mind that most animal nutritionists do not work with wildlife. They typically formulate and test pet food and develop effective feeding programs for domestic animal species. Researching the field and seeing what career options are available for animal nutritionists is essential. To learn more about what my organization does for conservation and education visit *www. sandiegozoo.org*. However, the best way to get formal exposure to nutrition, along with other disciplines related to animal care, is to enroll in an animal science program.

WHAT HAS BEEN YOUR BIGGEST ACCOMPLISHMENT?

Perhaps the most significant contributions made were in relation to giant pandas, both here in San Diego and in the People's Republic of China. We developed new feeding regimes for this species based on their biology, digestive system, and our knowledge of animal nutrition. This had a significant impact on the health of pandas at facilities that implemented the new diets. Continuing that theme, we evaluated the diets used to feed young pandas and helped to develop a revised rearing protocol that increased the survival of giant panda cubs partially or entirely raised in a nursery environment. Overall, one of our most significant accomplishments has been to demonstrate the benefits of actively managing animal diets, rather than just allowing them to occur, and the role that a professionally trained nutritionist can have in that process.

BONUS POINTS	EDUCATION	ON THE WEB	RELATED CAREERS
	BS, zoology; PhD, animal science, comparative animal nutrition emphasis	Zoological Society of San Diego (*www.sandiegozoo. org*); American Zoo and Aquarium Association (*http://aza.org*)	keeper, aquarist, wildlife rehabilitator, conservation biologist, veterinary technician, animal curator, animal health product sales

AQUACULTURE VETERINARIAN

If your pet fish has a deep, infected cut, an aquaculture veterinarian may suggest a topical treatment in conjunction with antibiotics, followed by stitches. Fish doctor Roy P. E. Yanong offers nutrition recommendations, diagnoses diseases, and performs physicals as he examines the overall health of his patients. Mostly Yanong works with ornamental fish farms that produce fish primarily for aquarium stores and hobbyists, but he also helps pet owners, teaches students, and participates in a range of nonprofit, state, and federal studies. Work for Yanong is one big aquarium, and he cannot imagine doing anything else.

DESCRIBE YOUR WORK.

I am a diagnostician and extension veterinarian for the University of Florida (UF). A typical day can vary. Because I run a fish disease diagnostic laboratory, I am always working with fish producers who have disease problems in their facilities or who seek advice on protocols to prevent disease. The main focus of producers is "herd" health. While an aquarium hobbyist considers the well-being of his or her pet, a farmer of pet fish is caring for hundreds to thousands of fish, so practicality and cost play a large part in treatment. For instance, I probably will not topically treat and stitch up 10,000 or 100,000 fish!

If a producer has a sick group of fish, I visit the facility to gather background information, which includes checking protocols, systems, water quality,

nutrition, and the present state of the fish. Often, a disease problem stems from husbandry or water quality. Fish are brought back to the laboratory for more complete assessments, including necropsies, microbiology, and preparation for histology. Once I determine the cause of disease, I work with the producer to remedy the situation and prevent similar problems in the future. I also offer fish health management programs, which include lectures and laboratories.

Part of my day is spent as an extension specialist answering questions regarding fish health. I help state agencies with fish health management, examine fish used in stock enhancement programs for overall health prior to release, and write articles for producers and the general public. Although the primary mission of my facility is working with producers, I often help hobbyists with sick fish find local veterinarians.

In addition, I oversee research projects that can range from vaccine development work to clinical drug trials against different parasites to studies on specific disease-causing organisms. I also mentor veterinary students interested in fish medicine by teaching courses related to fish health, acting as an adviser on specific research projects, and offering work opportunities in my laboratory.

Roy Yanong focuses on "herd" health.

WHAT SCIENCE IS NEEDED?

Aquatic veterinarians must be familiar with the basic biology of fish—anatomy, physiology, reproduction [normal and abnormal], and optimal husbandry requirements—and be able to distinguish between normals for different species and families of fish. We must understand the pathogenesis of infectious and noninfectious diseases, in short, how fish become sick. Specifically, this means knowing the interactions between the health of the fish and its homeostasis and immune system, the environment, and different pathogens [disease-causing agents]. Being familiar with disease-causing agents requires understanding the epidemiology of disease, the pathology [gross and histological] and pathophysiology of disease, microbiology, and immunology [including vaccines].

We must have pharmacology knowledge, such as how different chemical treatments enter and work within the fish to help fight or target a specific disease or disease-causing organism [such as bacteria,

parasite, fungus, or virus], how these treatments are metabolized by fish, and drug interactions. It is also necessary to understand how different parameters of water chemistry affect the health of fish. Finally, we must be aware of nutritional requirements and other issues related to fish health.

HOW DID YOU CHOOSE THIS FIELD?

I grew up in a family of medical doctors, which strongly influenced my interest in medicine and my passion to become a veterinarian. As an undergraduate, instead of working with the usual domestic animals such as dogs and cats, I was interested in working with agriculture, zoo, wildlife, aquarium, or aquaculture species.

After college I participated in a summer program, Aquavet, where I learned the basics of aquatic animal medicine, which included invertebrates, fish, sea turtles, aquatic birds, and marine mammals. I went on to study aquatic medicine in vet school with the understanding that

20

job opportunities for aquatic vets were limited. To broaden my experience, I formed an aquatic vet club with classmates and reached out to aquatic vet mentors. One such mentor, Dr. Greg Lewbart, directed me to a large fish farm in Florida that produced and imported tropical fish. I started working there after vet school as a staff veterinarian and was immediately immersed in the ornamental industry. I assisted with fish health management and diagnostics and had to learn my fish species very quickly. Four and a half years later I took my present job with UF to learn more about other aspects of the industry.

ADVICE FOR STUDENTS?

Students should make contact with the numerous vet schools that have fish or aquatic animal health programs. During college, courses in animal science and general biology are important, while other courses are required by vet schools for admission. Additionally, fish and aquatic animal health organizations want to foster interest in their fields and have student members.

A veterinary medical degree is required to learn the holistic approach and comparative aspects of health and disease. Prior to admission, most if not all vet schools require a certain number of volunteer or paid hours with a domestic animal vet, which is a great opportunity for an interested high school student to determine if vet school is a suitable path. While attending an accredited vet school, students are required to learn about all of the "traditional" species [such as cats, dogs, and cows] before focusing on "nontraditional" species [such as aquatic species].

To focus on aquatic medicine, a student must have both vet and aquatic animal experience. Aquatic experience includes keeping fish aquariums and understanding water quality, filtration, and husbandry, as well as working at a nearby public aquarium or aquaculture facility with a staff aquatic vet. Some high schools have integrated aquariums or aquaculture into their curricula; other districts have a magnet aquaculture school.

Good people skills, intuition, and excellent problem-solving abilities are essential to instill confidence in clients. Often, solutions are only found by asking the right questions and receiving honest answers—in vet lingo, we call this "getting the history."

BONUS POINTS	EDUCATION	ON THE WEB	RELATED CAREERS
	BS, molecular biophysics and biochemistry; VMD (most veterinary schools give the equivalent DVM.)	International Association for Aquatic Animal Medicine (*www.iaaam.org*); American Fisheries Society, Fish Health Section (*www. fisheries.org/fhs*)	commercial fisherman, underwater filmmaker, aquarium curator, environmental economist, baykeeper, aquaculture technician

Animal Kingdom

HONEY BEE SCIENTIST

It is common knowledge that honey bees collect nectar from flowers to make honey. But did you know honey is the only food we consume that is produced by insects? In addition, bees pollinate (fertilize) a staggering one-third of what we eat every day, including fruits and vegetables. Further, products of bees and their hives—such as honey and venom—are used internationally for antibiotic activity, bee-sting therapy, treating burn injuries, beauty products, and more. As an apiculturist, Eric Mussen studies honey bees and their relationships with the environment, people, and other organisms.

DESCRIBE THIS FIELD.

As a subspecialty of *entomology* [the scientific study of insects], *apiculture* [the science of beekeeping] focuses on honey bees. Most apiculturists, or bee scientists, in the United States are researchers at universities or in one of the four honey bee laboratories run by the U.S. Department of Agriculture (USDA). Areas of research include: honey bee genetics and breeding; honey bee diseases, parasites, and their control; honey bee nutrition; crop pollination using honey bees; rearing queen honey bees and manipulating eggs and semen for prolonged storage in liquid nitrogen; and medicinal uses of honey bee venom, honey, royal jelly [protein-rich substance fed to larvae], and propolis [resinous tree sap used as hive "glue"].

A few of us have partial or full appointments in extension apiculture, serving as liaisons between researchers and real-world beekeepers. Those

beekeepers may have one backyard colony [hobby beekeeping] or up to 70,000 colonies spread around the country in hundreds of apiary locations [commercial beekeeping].

FOCUS OF YOUR WORK?

As an extension apiculturist with the University of California, Davis, I enjoy helping real-world beekeepers keep their colonies as healthy and productive as possible. For instance, a colleague and I determined that a new antibiotic was useful for controlling a honey bee disease. Many commercial and hobby beekeepers now rely on our tested product to keep their bees alive.

Currently, I am involved in studies of various types of sugar syrups that are being fed to honey bee colonies. Some of the syrups, which used to work well, now are toxic to bees. We have to find the reason behind the toxicity and prevent further injury to bees. In addition to working with researchers and beekeepers, I provide bee-related information to federal and state regulatory agencies and industry groups.

PRODUCTS OF THE HIVE?

Honey is important to beekeepers as a source of income and is consumed by the general public [about 0.5 kg/person annually in the United States], mostly in processed foods. Honey is used extensively in foreign countries for burn and wound healing, and is being studied as a health food because of its antioxidants and possible help with cholesterol levels.

Bee-collected *pollen* is used as a human health supplement and fed back to the bees. Pollen is the "health food" for the bees, containing proteins, vitamins, minerals, and lipids essential for honey bee growth and development. Although few studies suggest that pollen actually helps in human nutrition, it is thought to possibly reduce problems with hay fever if collected in the local area.

Propolis is sticky, resinous material bees collect from trees [such as pine pitch], which has very strong antibiotic activity against bacteria, fungi, and viruses. The bees smear this gluelike substance on interior walls of hives for protection from the elements. The material is used quite frequently in complementary and alternative medicine for all sorts of maladies, such as gum disease.

Royal jelly is a blend of sugar and substances secreted from glands in the heads of worker bees.

Mussen helps beekeepers keep their colonies healthy and productive.

The jelly—rich in proteins, B-complex vitamins, and antibiotic properties—is used to feed larval workers and drones, and is fed in large quantities to adult queens. Some studies show a potential for royal jelly to relieve human maladies and increase youthful appearance.

Although a few people develop lethal allergic reactions to honey bee stings, a very large number of people rely on periodic bee-sting therapy, which uses *venom* to treat a variety of illnesses. Originally used for arthritis treatments in the United States, honey bee stings now are used like "hot needles" at acupuncture locations on the body. One of the most controversial treatments is for multiple sclerosis (MS). Many MS patients taking bee-sting therapy claim the stings increase peripheral circulation and cause MS remission, but conventional doctors are skeptical.

ADVICE FOR STUDENTS?

In general, students should take their education seriously because material and habits learned in high school will be used throughout life. If students have an idea of what they want to do in the future, they should begin to lay the groundwork. Because apiculture is a biological field, for instance, students should take a lot of life science courses.

Nearly all apiculturists have a doctorate in entomology or related science, with a research focus on honey bees. Most apiculturists are interested in insects fairly early in their lives and careers. I, however, did not think that honey bees would be my specific insect of focus. In graduate school, I was on the track to becoming an insect microbiologist when I was offered the opportunity to study virus diseases of honey bees.

Students interested in learning more about this field should contact scientists or professors and ask questions. When seeking advice or looking into undergraduate schools, institutions with entomology degree programs are good places to start. Also, colleges and universities close to USDA honey bee labs often form apiculture-research partnerships.

BONUS POINTS	EDUCATION	ON THE WEB	RELATED CAREERS
	BS, entomology; MS, entomology, minor in plant pathology; PhD, entomology, minor in microbiology	Eric Mussen *(entomology. ucdavis.edu/faculty/mussen. cfm)*; National Honey Board *(www.honey.com)*; BeeSource *(www.beesource. com)*	entomologist, pest control technician or assistant, apiarist (beekeeper, beekeeping assistant, or bee inspector), integrated pest management specialist

24

AQUATIC CONSERVATION BIOLOGIST

To protect the diversity of life on Earth, conservation biologists study species and habitats in danger of extinction. Freshwater is arguably one of the most critical global resources. The ecosystem biodiversity of this invaluable resource is highly threatened. In his role as an aquatic conservation biologist, Zeb Hogan travels the world to better understand and reduce threats to endangered freshwater fish and their habitats. Hogan's efforts support the invaluable freshwater biodiversity and ecosystem health.

FOCUS OF YOUR WORK?

My main project, National Geographic's Megafishes, focuses on the study and conservation of the world's giant freshwater fish [see photo]. On expeditions to some of Earth's most diverse freshwater ecosystems, I collect information about the life history, population status, geographic range, and threats associated with giant fish species. This information is synthesized into IUCN Red List assessments of threatened species. The assessments summarize population and distribution trends over time to determine extinction risk. While on missions, I meet with scientists and fishers, participate in biological studies and inventories, and talk with local people about their unique way of life. My principal goal is to investigate causes behind the global loss of freshwater biodiversity.

Locally, in the United States, I focus on the management of fish and their habitats in ecosystems such as Walker Lake, Nevada. Walker Lake is a desert lake becoming increasingly saline due to a combination of natural evaporation and extraction of water for agriculture. The lake is so saline that fish such as Lahontan cutthroat trout and tui chub struggle to survive. My research focuses on methods to improve the lake health and restore fish populations.

DESCRIBE A TYPICAL DAY.

Every day is different. When I am not in the field, I spend time in my university office [as an assistant research professor] responding to e-mails,

Hogan holding a 117 cm taimen—which have undergone massive declines due to habitat loss, pollution, and overfishing—in the Eg-Uur rive in northern Mongolia.

planning future expeditions, buying equipment, meeting with students, attending seminars, writing reports, submitting grants, and preparing scientific manuscripts. Once I am in the field, I spend almost all of my time on or near the water.

In Southeast Asia, most of my field sites are near populated areas, so my team boards in hotels and relies on local fishers to help gather information. In Cambodia, for instance, we stay in the city of Phnom Penh and take a small boat along the river twice a day. While on the river, we interview fishers about their catches and the abundance of endangered species. If fishers catch an endangered fish, we work with them to tag and release the fish.

Alternatively, in Central Asia's Mongolia we live in Mongolian *yurts* [tentlike structures], eat traditional food, and rely on solar energy to power our equipment. The temperature can drop to well below 0°C late in the season, so it is sometimes a challenge just to keep ourselves and our equipment

in good condition. There, we work with recreational fishers to gather information about the ecology of the world's largest trout. Our days are spent on the river tagging and releasing fish, and our nights taking care of work-related chores [such as charging batteries, entering data in a computer, fixing equipment, making calls by satellite phone].

Aside from office and fieldwork, I also write articles, speak at seminars, and work with the National Geographic Society to produce television news stories and shows. Sharing stories with a broader audience helps raise awareness about the existence and conservation status of endangered freshwater fish.

ANY ADVICE FOR STUDENTS?

Students can start thinking about subjects that excite them and reflecting on what, specifically, they enjoy about those subjects. For example, students interested in ecology should try to figure out *why*. Is it because they like being outside or asking and answering scientific questions? In my case, I have always been curious about the natural world and I enjoy learning about that world through field studies.

In high school, I read news stories and books about ecology and conservation. Eager to get out in the field, I sent letters to aquariums around the country inquiring about summer internships and applied for a summer field course on natural resources management. Most universities have research assistant positions available to undergraduates, so it was easier to get involved in the field once I was a college student at the University of Arizona. I worked as a field tech with the Arizona Fish and Wildlife Research Cooperative every summer until I graduated.

In all, I followed a traditional path for an academic research scientist. Upon receiving a bachelor's degree in ecology and evolutionary biology, I participated as an exchange student in the Fulbright Program in Thailand, attained a doctorate in ecology, and then continued as a post-doctoral fellow. While not all students need to follow this exact path, it is important for aspiring conservation biologists to receive good grades [especially in science classes] and have a relatively well-articulated idea of their research interests.

JOB SATISFACTION?

I love the freedom to direct the focus of my research, which has developed and evolved over time. I am always challenged by a novel question or problem and almost every day I learn something new. For instance, I recently started working with the United Nations Convention on Migratory Species. As part of this work, I am learning all about sharks, which were previously unfamiliar to me.

From a scientific perspective, the most exciting moments often come with an answer to a question about the behavior or life history of a poorly studied animal. For example, I worked for quite some time trying to determine how far *Pangasius krempfi* [a type of catfish] migrate up the Mekong River in Southeast Asia. We finally discovered that the catfish actually behave like salmon and migrate about 1,000 km upstream. Findings such as this are inspiring not only because they are breakthroughs, but also because the information may help protect the species. As for personal satisfaction, it is incredible to work in beautiful and remote areas and realize such places still exist.

BONUS POINTS	EDUCATION BS, ecology and evolutionary biology; PhD, ecology	ON THE WEB Society for Conservation Biology *(www.conbio.org)*; International Union for Conservation of Nature and Natural Resources (IUCN) Red List of Threatened Species *(www.iucnredlist.org)*	RELATED CAREERS marine biologist, aquatic chemist, physical oceanographer, aquaculture veterinarian, environmental consultant

Animal Kingdom

OYSTER WRANGLER

Did you know that oysters, simply by eating, filter the water they live in? An adult oyster can filter up to 225 L of water every day! In addition, oyster reefs play the important role of sheltering many fish and crab species. Today, the Chesapeake Bay's oyster population is dangerously low—down to only a few percent of its historic level. To improve the overall health of the bay, we need to restore these water-purifying, habitat-providing marine animals. As an Oyster Restoration and Fisheries Scientist with the Chesapeake Bay Foundation (CBF), Stephanie Reynolds supports this important ecological resource.

OVERVIEW OF THE WORK.

My job with CBF involves two distinct, but related, activities: fieldwork and lobbying. Fieldwork entails joining forces with volunteers and partner organizations to build reefs—out of shell or artificial substrate [for example, crushed recycled concrete]—and plant oysters in the bay. Oysters filter pollutants by consuming them or shaping them into small packets, which are then deposited on the bay's floor. Their reef structures provide habitat for many other species, such as blue crabs, striped bass, weakfish, blue fish, white perch, croaker, black drum, and spotted sea trout. At one point, oysters in the bay could filter about 70 trillion L of water in a week's time; today, because of declining oyster populations, it would take the remaining oysters more than a year to filter that same amount.

As a lobbyist, my role is to be the voice of the bay, specifically of all its marine animals. For marine animals to survive, conservation-oriented laws and regulations must exist to protect their habitat. State legislature and government agencies are constantly reworking the laws and regulations that dictate how many marine animals can be harvested from the bay, what equipment can be used to harvest them, and even broader topics that affect water quality. CBF tracks all of the proposed laws and regulations, and educates decision makers. Lawmakers are not scientists, so they often need help recognizing how a particular law might impact the bay and other natural resources.

FINDING A NICHE.

I grew up sailing on the bay, and I care deeply about its health. I studied science writing as an undergraduate, with a minor in biology [so I was not technically a science major]. After college, I

28

spent eight years as a professional sailor, working my way up from deckhand to captain. During that time, I worked on boats that took students out to study marine biology, which led me to feel even more invested in protecting the marine environment. When it was time to find a lifestyle that did not require living out of a duffle bag, I looked to my home port: the Chesapeake Bay.

Once I recognized my desire to work in the marine sciences, I decided to pursue a master's degree. Before applying to graduate school, however, I had to take several prerequisite science courses that were not part of my undergraduate program. When I finished graduate school, I took my current job with the CBF. I love that I can be outside, especially on the water, while helping the environment.

ADVICE FOR STUDENTS.

When considering a career, students should follow their passions. Those interested in marine science should get experience on the water through a swim team, canoeing, fishing, or a summer job as a tour-boat deckhand, for instance. Getting involved in extracurricular activities related to the environment—such as volunteering with a conservation organization, joining an ecology club, or starting a recycling program at school—shows leadership and a true commitment to helping our natural world.

To follow a traditional marine science track [such as university-based research], graduate degrees are typically necessary. However, a lot of

Reynolds plants oysters to improve the bay's health.

careers related to marine science exist that do not require advanced degrees. The policy work I do—which can be done with a bachelor's degree—calls for biology knowledge, but also a connection with people and the ability to communicate complex ideas clearly. Entry-level field technicians require a bachelor's degree in the sciences [and work outside most days!].

MAKING A DIFFERENCE.

I think one of the best things about my job is the feedback I get when working with volunteers. So many people want to do something positive for the environment—to make a difference—and they just do not know how. Sometimes that includes legislators who want to pass good laws to protect the bay, but who need help understanding what issues to tackle. I am able to guide those people to do things that can help.

The one issue that can be difficult to handle in my line of work is the magnitude of degradation in our marine environment. Millions of people live in its watershed, and all of their pollution runs down into the bay. It can be staggering to think about. I just have to keep believing that I am helping in some small way: a healthy oyster reef here, a volunteer with a new interest in environmental stewardship there. My brightest hope is that the generation now in high school has had more environmental education than any generation in history. Today's students will be the lawmakers, business people, and scientists of tomorrow!

BONUS POINTS	EDUCATION BS, science writing, biology minor; MS, environmental science	ON THE WEB Chesapeake Bay Foundation (*www.cbf.org*)	RELATED CAREERS marine-science technician, environmental planner, baykeeper, environmental lawyer, aquaculture veterinarian, ecotourism guide, underwater filmmaker

SHARK ADVOCATE

Most sharks are the top predators in their ecosystems, yet they are often at the bottom of the conservation priority list. Because they are underprotected and exceptionally slow growing, and therefore vulnerable to overfishing, most of the world's shark populations are declining. In fact, 20% are threatened with extinction. To restore shark populations within the lifetimes of today's high school students, action is needed now. Sonja Fordham—the Policy Director for the Shark Alliance and Shark Conservation Program at the Ocean Conservancy—enjoys sticking up for these underdogs. Fordham believes the public, including students and teachers, are the key to turning this situation around.

OVERVIEW OF THE FIELD.

Shark advocates spend a majority of their time trying to convince officials at various levels of government that sharks are important, valuable, and deserving of conservation action. Sharks are essential for maintaining balance in marine ecosystems; offer insight into combating human diseases; and are a source for food, income, and recreation for people around the world. In order to provide these benefits, shark populations must be protected from overfishing.

Because my organization is a science-based advocacy group, I focus on translating advice from scientists and other technical experts into public policy. This involves distilling scientists' recommendations and transforming those points into language that the average citizen can understand and the average fishery manager can absorb in a limited amount of time. If we convey information that makes sense and if necessary actions are supported by the public, we hope that fishery managers will act. Usually this action takes the form of restrictions on fishing, habitat use, or trade.

SUPPORTING SHARKS.

Seventeen years ago—when I accepted a job in the fisheries program at the Center for Marine Conservation [now called Ocean Conservancy]—I had secret hopes of eventually transferring into the program focused on marine mammals, my high school passion. When I got "inside," however, and saw how the save-the-fish mail stacked up against the save-the-whales mail [not well] and how marine-fish restrictions compared to marine-mammal protections, I decided that fish were more in need of advocates and stayed put.

Fordham enjoys sticking up for sharks.

only issues related to conservation of sharks and closely related skates and rays. I enjoy being on the forefront of untraditional campaigns. I also like the great variety of tasks and audiences that are associated with my job.

A TYPICAL DAY?

My day-to-day tasks are dominated by writing projects. I craft a lot of letters to government officials at state through global levels requesting safeguards for sharks—usually limits on shark fishing. To foster public awareness and support for these requests, I also write action alerts (to prompt our members to send letters to policy makers at major decision points), press releases, fact sheets, opinion pieces, magazine articles, testimony, in-depth reports, technical papers for scientific or legal journals, petitions, and text for cartoons and children's publications. Even an invitation to a reception [such as to launch a report or campaign] has to be carefully worded to optimize its impact.

At the time, the wasteful and indefensible practice of shark finning—slicing off a shark's valuable fins for soup and discarding the body at sea—was still legal throughout the world, and fisheries targeting sharks off the U.S. East Coast were expanding without any restrictions whatsoever. As sharks generally grow slowly, mature late, and produce few offspring, it is easy to see how the situation amounted to a recipe for disaster.

Since then, I have done my best to make people realize that sharks are as vulnerable and deserving of effective protections as whales and dolphins. As the Ocean Conservancy's fish conservation program expanded, I pared down my responsibilities to

My other main role is to directly appeal to people and decision makers through meetings with members of congress, parliament, and government administrations; special events; presentations at scientific conferences; rallies; and other speaking engagements. As part of this work, it is important to keep up to date on scientific developments, government proposals, and other news related to sharks, and to maintain cooperative working relationships with conservationists, supporters, scientists, government officials, industry, and the media.

32

BACKGROUND NEEDED?

I truly believe that it takes people from all walks of life to form effective coalitions. Naturally, a background in science [or law] is extremely helpful in building a career as an advocate for sharks and wildlife. I cannot understate, however, the importance of developing strong writing skills. So much of advocacy work involves writing, and there is a great need for people who can craft clear, succinct documents for a variety of audiences [from children to elected officials to scientists to journalists]. This is the number one skill I look for when considering prospective interns and employees.

I received a bachelor's degree in marine science. For many years, I expected that I would return for a graduate degree, but never found a time when I did not love my work enough to leave it or thought the sharks could fend for themselves! I am very fortunate to have found a wonderful, ever-changing, and challenging job at a great organization. I am happy about where my on-the-job training has taken me and honored that at least one of my publications has been used in graduate-level science courses to uncover the realities of the fisheries management process.

ANY ADVICE FOR STUDENTS?

I often wish I had studied public speaking and joined the debate club when I was in high school. Such endeavors can help to build confidence and serve as a strong foundation for any advocate. In the end, I believe the most important qualities are passion for the cause, tenacity, creativity, integrity, and respect for others' perspectives. A sense of humor can also help one through the tough times.

Students have the power to dramatically improve the outlook for sharks. Citizens of all ages should remember that their government officials work for and need to hear from them. A simple letter of concern, especially a personal one, can help to demonstrate support for shark conservation and spur decision makers into action. Such pressure represents the sharks' best hope—perhaps their only hope—for a brighter future.

BONUS POINTS	EDUCATION	ON THE WEB	RELATED CAREERS
	BS, marine science	Shark Alliance (www.sharkalliance.org); Ocean Conservancy (www.oceanconservancy.org)	marine-science technician, environmental planner, baykeeper, environmental lawyer, aquaculture veterinarian, ecotourism guide, underwater filmmaker

ARTISTIC ENDEAVORS

Artistic Endeavors

SCIENTIFIC ILLUSTRATOR

If you have an eye for nature's details—such as the way some petals of a flower catch sunlight or how its stem is covered in tiny hairs—then you may be a good candidate for a career in scientific illustration. This career requires careful observation to create images of subjects such as animals, plants, insects—and in Lynette R. Cook's case, outer space. Drawings, paintings, three-dimensional models, and computer graphics help viewers learn more about the subject at hand. Scientific illustration should not only inform people but also inspire them and help them appreciate the natural world.

WHAT IS YOUR WORK LIKE?

Before I illustrate a subject, I gather information from my client, tap into my own knowledge bank, and do any research necessary to learn more, such as consult with scientists, science writers, and editors. I then create imagery that is scientifically correct, visually appealing, and appropriate for the intended audience [such as students, the general public, or science professionals].

The images can be found in books, magazines, scientific papers, posters, the internet, and even PowerPoint presentations. One ongoing project involves working with The California and Carnegie Planet Search team to illustrate planets they have discovered outside our solar system. These extrasolar planets are detected by indirect means—such as observation of a neighboring star's motion and brightness—and therefore can be visually portrayed only through artwork. A scientist tells me the type of star neighboring an extrasolar planet, the distance between the star and planet, and the planet's mass. These facts give me information about the color of both celestial bodies and whether the planet might be large and gaseous like Jupiter or smaller, dry, and rocky like Mercury. After doing some additional research, I try to create an accurate and aesthetically pleasing illustration of the new planet. Learning about extrasolar planets before they are publicly announced is exciting, as is showing through my artwork what these worlds might look like up close.

36

WHAT IS YOUR BACKGROUND?

I have always loved both art and science. In high school, when I began to think about college and a career, I had trouble choosing one field over another. As an undergraduate and, back then, an overachiever, I majored in both painting and drawing and biology. I also attended a summer workshop held by the Guild of Natural Science Illustrators (GNSI). The workshop was my first formal training in scientific illustration, which combined my two areas of interest into one profession. I went on to graduate school for a master's degree in drawing with a specialization in scientific illustration. During college and graduate school, I didn't expect to end up in the field of astronomy and therefore focused on biology, botany, and zoology. Once I started working with celestial subjects, I took some astronomy courses at a local community college to expand my knowledge.

ANY ADVICE FOR STUDENTS?

Students can visit GNSI online *(www.gnsi.org)* to learn more about related careers, workshops, and lectures. The International Association of Astronomical Artists website *(www.iaaa.org)* is a good resource for information about space art specifically. Although a science degree is not required in this field, greater subject knowledge makes an illustrator's job easier. Students interested in outer space should enroll in astronomy courses. For those who like plants, botany classes are helpful. Because computer programs are used for sketching and final artwork, digital knowledge and skills are needed. However, it is also very important to have conventional drawing and painting abilities. A final product might be digital, traditional, or a combination of the two. To practice essential observation and artistic skills, students should create realistic illustrations of objects. For example, if a student paints a bird, he or she must carefully study and accurately record subtle details: its beak, leg, and wing proportions and range of colors, highlights, and shadows.

BONUS POINTS	EDUCATION	ON THE WEB	RELATED CAREERS
	BS, biology; BFA, drawing and painting; MFA, drawing, scientific illustration specialization	International Association of Astronomical Artists *(www. iaaa.org);* Guild of Natural Science Illustrators *(www. gnsi.org)*	landscape architect, medical illustrator, science journalist, scientific photographer, art conservator

ART CONSERVATIONIST

Conservation scientists gather clues and evidence with scientific tools to help curators and conservators uncover mysteries of art such as age and authenticity. M. Susan Barger sees herself as a pathologist of art objects—she biopsies material for research, determines what went wrong, and then gives a diagnosis for treatment. As she investigates the best way to care for an object, Barger must consider science, art techniques, and materials history.

DESCRIBE YOUR WORK.

Conservation scientists conduct research to evaluate the chemical, optical, mechanical, and physical properties of historic and artistic objects. We gather information that can help restore, conserve, and care for artwork, using various tools such as x-rays to scan for cracks, infrared cameras to look beneath painted surfaces for underdrawings and original plans, and microscopes to examine tiny fragments of material. We examine the physical, biological, and chemical effects of temperature, humidity, light, and pollutants on different materials. The research allows us to determine the condition of objects, the need for treatment or conservation, and the best methods for preservation. With the resulting information, we advise curators and art conservators on the best way to stabilize, conserve, and care for artwork.

Currently, as a research consultant, I am asked to analyze objects and answer particular questions for a curator or art dealer such as "What is this object made of?" "Is the object as old as it is purported to be?" "Is it stable?" and "What is making this object fail?" I identify materials, attempt to understand how they age, and determine what that means to the care of art and heritage materials. Once these analyses are done, I deliver reports to a client, detailing my findings.

HOW DID YOU CHOOSE THIS FIELD?

In high school, I loved both science and art. I thought I could major in art and chemistry in college, but I was advised not to do this and instead obtained a double degree in art and French. When I was 24 years old, I went back to school for a master's in fine arts. However, my desire to involve more chemistry in my studies led to my dismissal from art school; I was told, "Science destroys creativity." Determined that science and creativity were not so unrelated, I spent a summer soul-searching and returned to school, this time for graduate studies in photographic science. I then went on to receive an interdisciplinary doctorate in materials science, chemistry, and history of technology. When I got my degree, very few scientists had pursued scientific doctoral research using art objects and artifacts as subjects. I knew early on that I did not want to work on objects the way a conservator does, but I realized the need for people who could merge science and art to solve problems for conservators.

WHAT SKILLS ARE NEEDED?

To analyze a piece of art, you need to be a good scientist and know a great deal about not only art but also the technology and history of materials. This knowledge is crucial when working with art professionals in order to understand what problems you are being asked to solve. Curators, conservators, or art dealers may not be able to describe their needs in scientific language. Conservation scientists often must pinpoint questions and communicate findings in a way that clients understand.

WHY IS THIS CAREER UNIQUE?

Conservation science presents very interesting and difficult problems that have to be approached in special ways—you cannot take large samples from a precious painting or take a chunk out of a sculpture to perform an analysis. And when determining how to care for a work of art, you must deal with the original material as it is, not how you wish it would be. The materials in some artwork may be unstable, but they are part of the object and not something you can change.

BONUS POINTS	EDUCATION	ON THE WEB	RELATED CAREERS
	BA, art, French; PhD, materials science, chemistry, and history of technology	The American Institute for Conservation of Historic and Artistic Works (*http://aic.stanford.edu*)	curator, museum technician, forensics technician, pharmaceutical analyst, historic preservation scientist

Artistic Endeavors

LANDSCAPE ARCHITECT

From planning the layout of a zoo to recreating wetlands affected by a development project, landscape architects use a blend of science and art to design outdoor spaces. As a consultant for the restoration of natural sites, Brandon DeRosa strives to balance beauty, nature, and functionality in his designs so they consider the needs of people and the environment.

DESCRIBE WHAT YOU DO.

We may design areas such as parks, campuses, and resorts, or plan the restoration of natural sites such as wetlands and forested land. Whether the project involves a public development or natural habitat, the shared objective is to meet public needs while respecting the environment. With my background in science and design, I have created a niche uncommon in this profession best described as a habitat restoration specialist. I often work on several projects simultaneously, and my role changes from landscape architect to wetland biologist depending on the project. Working closely with other designers, scientists, and engineers, I am typically involved in the planning stages of a project, but opportunities also exist to partake in the design's construction. There is no typical day in the office—one day I might work on a restoration design at my desk and the next day I might fly to Alaska to do wetland assessment. Every design I work on requires hours of thought on so many different levels it is like being an artist with the landscape as my canvas. Each object in the design serves a purpose and reflects the overall design concept.

WHY LANDSCAPE ARCHITECTURE?

My love of the outdoors and design inspirations can be traced back to my childhood. Early on I appreciated landscape form as something I could manipulate to make more interesting—I remember one winter, when I was about 8 years old, digging trails through fresh snow in my backyard and admiring the contrast between white mounds and green grass. In high school, my two favorite subjects were science and art. Unaware of a career that combined these interests, I decided to pursue a bachelor's degree in natural resource management, which allowed me to study all of the biological sciences. Throughout college I worked for my uncle's

40

business, which focused on designing and creating large-scale wetland environments. I achieved a solid science background and found wetland biology fascinating, but I had no outlet for my creative tendencies. In my final year of college I took some art-related electives. With this revived energy in the arts and advice from professors, I decided to study landscape architecture in graduate school.

A CURRENT PROJECT?

I am working as an environmental mitigation inspector for one of the largest public-funded projects in Washington—the third runway for the Seattle-Tacoma International Airport. So how does a landscape architect get involved in a runway project? As you can imagine, creating a more than two-mile-long runway may have some environmental impacts. Compensatory wetland mitigation involves the creation or restoration of new wetland to offset the loss of a wetland affected by a development project. In this way, the functions provided by a wetland, such as flood control, wildlife habitat, and natural filtration, are maintained in the environment. By overseeing this mitigation and partici-

Brandon DeRosa's profession blends science and art.

pating in its construction, I am actually building something tangible beyond a design on paper. Being involved in the end result is very fulfilling.

ANY ADVICE FOR STUDENTS?

Students interested in art, science, and the environment in particular should find a landscape architect or firm in the phone book, call them, explain your interest in the field, and ask to see some of their designs. Most landscape architects love nothing better than to showcase and discuss their work—not to say we are vain, but more so passionate. Visit *www. asla.org* to learn more about this occupation. People of all types enter this profession. I believe the common thread is the desire to create aesthetically pleasing environments.

BONUS POINTS	EDUCATION	ON THE WEB	RELATED CAREERS
	BS, natural resources; MS, landscape architecture; registered landscape architect	American Society of Landscape Architects (*www.asla.org*)	landscape gardener, horticultural technician, architect, wetland biologist, forester, environmental scientist, park naturalist, habitat restoration specialist

Artistic Endeavors

MUSICAL ACOUSTICS SCIENTIST

When we think of sound, several things come to mind, from irritating noises to our favorite songs. Musical acoustics is the scientific study of sound as it relates to music. Some musical acousticians research how instruments work and how they can be improved, others investigate how we perceive and think about music and musical sounds. James Beauchamp has developed computer programs that produce musical sounds similar to those created by instruments—in essence, virtual instruments. Because of scientists such as Beauchamp, computer music has evolved from only abstract layers of sound, to sounds that include replicas of real instruments.

HOW DID YOU BECOME A MUSICAL SCIENTIST?

In high school, I thought I might become a composer, but I was also very interested in math and physical science. So, as an undergraduate, I decided to major in electrical engineering—but I kept up music as a hobby, playing the trumpet in jazz bands. While working on my master's degree in electrical engineering, I started to explore the idea of using electronics to synthesize musical instrument sounds and produce music. Fortunately, an opportunity to work on a doctorate in electronic music opened up at the University of Illinois (UI), supported by a grant from the Magnavox Company. Following my graduate studies, I joined the UI electrical engineering faculty to teach undergraduate and graduate students musical acoustics, electronic

and computer music, and audio engineering. There, I also continued to work on sound analysis and synthesis—creating electronic models [computer programs] that produce authentic musical sounds—under a National Science Foundation grant.

DESCRIBE YOUR WORK.

Although musical acoustics is highly interdisciplinary, some core knowledge exists that just about all musical acousticians share, which is explained in most books on musical acoustics, such as Thomas Rossing's *The Science of Sound* (1982). First, there is basic physical acoustics, which consists of simple and not-so-simple vibrators that generate sinusoidal and complex waveforms; wave propagation in media such as air, liquids, and solids; and spectral and modal analysis, which is the

42

theory of frequency analysis. Frequencies are the "atoms" that make up sounds. Sometimes we are strongly aware of them as pitches but often they are "buried" in the sound itself and only become part of the sound's texture or *timbre*. The second type of core knowledge relates to the theory of hearing, which attempts to explain how the ear works and the relationship of pitch, loudness, and timbre [sound quality] to frequency, intensity, and sound spectrum. Finally, there is the acoustics of musical instruments, which is based on physical acoustics. Beyond this core knowledge, musical acousticians may have further training in topics such as recording, reproduction, and electronic and computer music.

CONTRIBUTIONS TO SCIENCE AND MUSIC.

I retired as a professor about 10 years ago, but I continue to work in musical acoustics—I enjoy both science and music and challenges associated with this field. For instance, I advise and collaborate with graduate students on their thesis work, which usually corresponds to my research.

Most of my research has focused on computer models for analysis, synthesis [production], and perception of musical timbre. For example, with one student, I developed a software program [called Music 4C] that synthesizes music and thereby allows users to compose music on the computer with virtual instruments.

ANY ADVICE FOR STUDENTS?

As undergraduates, most musical acoustics scientists major in physics; a few major in music, psychology, or computer science. Students interested in working in this field should study physics, math, computer programming, and music—music should at least be a hobby—and explore colleges or universities with programs related to musical acoustics. Most musical acoustics scientists are familiar with making physical measurements, writing computer programs, conducting perceptual studies, and critically listening to music.

BONUS POINTS	EDUCATION BS, MS, PhD, electrical engineering	ON THE WEB Acoustical Society of America (*http://asa.aip.org*); Exploratorium's Science of Music (*www.exploratorium. edu/music*); Beauchamp's web page (*http://ems.music. uiuc.edu/beaucham*)	RELATED CAREERS architectural acoustician, speech pathologist, music theorist, ethnomusicologist, sociomusicologist

ENVIRONMENTAL ISSUES

ENVIRONMENTAL CONSULTANT

Asbestos has been used for centuries in countless building products because of its strength, flexibility, and heat resistance. In the late 1960s, however, evidence emerged that this versatile material was a dangerous health risk. Along with such dangerous materials as lead-based paint and mold, asbestos is now one of the potential hazards environmental consultants search for inside schools, hospitals, and other properties. While assessing building safety, these investigators also look for outside sources of contamination, such as petroleum or chemical leakage from underground storage tanks. As an environmental consultant with Facility Engineering Associates, Maureen Roskoski works to keep the public safe from environmental hazards.

DESCRIBE YOUR JOB.

When a company or individual wants to purchase a property, but needs to know the potential environmental concerns before closing the deal, they come to me for an assessment. I start with a complete historical review of the property to determine its past uses. For example, if an office building was built in an urban area in 1980, I figure out what existed on that same property prior to that year. I review aerial photographs, fire insurance maps, and city directories. If a gas station or a dry cleaner resided on the property during the 1950s or 1970s, there is cause for environmental concern. Improper historical practices may have resulted in soil or groundwater contamination. I also check

state and federal databases for surrounding sites that could contaminate the property.

Many factors come into play when determining if an off-site area may have caused contamination, such as the geology and hydrogeology of the area, the type and extent of contamination identified at the site, and the topographic gradient. If I identify a potential environmental concern, I recommend further investigation, which usually consists of performing soil and groundwater sampling. In these tests, wells are drilled into the ground, soil and water samples are collected and analyzed by a lab, and a corrective action plan is prepared. The historical data and off-site information are pooled with my assessment of the property's indoor

46

contaminants, such as radon or mold.

To expose potential hazards within a building, I use sampling methods and evaluate action levels—the degree of a harmful toxin that requires medical surveillance, increased industrial hygiene monitoring, or biological monitoring—based on scientific studies and data. The work I am most proud of involves projects in which I help someone and make a difference. For instance, I did a survey of a public building and found asbestos pipe insulation in very poor condition. No one in the building was aware of this potential hazard, and these residents were being exposed to a cancer-causing agent on a daily basis. My company helped the building get rid of the asbestos and left the property in much better shape.

ANY ADVICE FOR STUDENTS?

There are many paths in the environmental industry for all education levels, from technicians with high school educations, to environmental engineers with undergraduate degrees, to industrial hygienists with master's degrees, and senior consultants with doctorates. To learn more about different options, students can visit the Environmental

Maureen Roskoski makes sure properties don't pose environmental hazards.

Careers Organization online at *www.eco.org*. My undergraduate degree is in environmental Earth science with a strong biology emphasis. I originally wanted to be a marine biologist, but when grad school did not pan out I took a job as an environmental consultant—and here I am today. I have learned a lot about my profession through on-the-job training and through several outside classes required for asbestos and lead work. However, my undergraduate education—from lab techniques to problem solving—taught me about scientific process, and I use that knowledge every day.

BONUS POINTS	EDUCATION BS, environmental Earth science	ON THE WEB Environmental Careers Organization *(www.eco.org)*	RELATED CAREERS groundwater engineer, industrial hygienist, wetland biologist, geologist, ecologist

OCEANOGRAPHER

From exploring tides and waves to investigating the chemical properties and age of seawater, oceanographers use their knowledge of several basic science fields to study the world's oceans and coastal waters. Evan Forde, at the National Oceanic and Atmospheric Administration (NOAA), has amassed 17 months at sea during his career. Forde, recognized by NOAA in 1979 as the first African American oceanographer to participate in dives aboard research submersibles [vessels that can submerge and operate underwater], tackles unsolved mysteries. His research contributes toward understanding and improving the delicate relationship between people and our planet.

HOW DID YOU BECOME AN OCEANOGRAPHER?

I always wanted to be a scientist. I already had a telescope, microscope, and chemistry set by the time I was in third grade. Swimming and other water sports have always been preferable pastimes, and *The Undersea World of Jacques Cousteau* television show particularly inspired me. In high school I took an elective environmental oceanography science course and began to entertain the idea of actually becoming an oceanographer. My teacher was an avid scuba diver and always had interesting ways to help us understand the undersea world. One day my teacher released a live crab into our octopus-inhabited classroom aquarium. The octopus eventually ate the crab, but we were stunned that the crab, while defending itself, cut off two of the octopus's tentacles before he was subdued

and consumed. I was fascinated, entertained, and hooked. I went on to receive my bachelor's degree in geology and my master's degree in marine geology and geophysics. I have worked for NOAA since 1973.

PLEASE DESCRIBE A TYPICAL DAY AT WORK.

In the laboratory I am typically using a computer and examining ocean samples. I write proposals to formulate research plans, plot and analyze data, and detail the results of my completed work in documents to be published in scientific journals.

The working environment at sea can be demanding. I have used sound to map the ocean floor and subsurface sediment layers, taken air and water samples to monitor pollutants and carbon dioxide levels, used optical devices to scan the deep

48

ocean layers for evidence of underwater volcanoes, and taken thousands of samples of deep-sea sediments and rocks.

WHAT HAS BEEN YOUR SCARIEST EXPERIENCE?

Submersible dives are the most exhilarating and scariest experiences I have had, not only in my occupation, but also in my life. During one dive, a small, underwater landslide on top of the submersible ALVIN trapped us nearly two miles beneath the surface. [The pressure at that depth was approximately 1800 kg/6.5 cm^2.] For about 12 minutes, it was unclear if we would ever be able to free the sub and surface.

While I always have a few butterflies in my stomach before every dive, being in a submersible and exploring depths seen by few humans is an awesome experience. Very few organisms, aside from some beautiful bioluminescent creatures, have adapted to conditions in the deep dark ocean.

ADVICE FOR STUDENTS?

Diverse science courses such as physics, chemistry, biology, and geology are essential for potential

Evan Forde finds exploring depths an awesome experience.

oceanographers. Good writing skills are often underemphasized, but are essential for any scientific researcher. Students should know basic computer programming, logic, and mathematics to manipulate, plot, and analyze data. Students should also search the internet for oceanographers working on projects of interest, e-mail them, and ask them to answer specific questions.

A student interested in an oceanography-related college track should try to visit and tour an actual oceanographic research facility. I would strongly recommend that any potential scientist actually work in a research facility, as an intern or unpaid volunteer, to get a feel for the day-to-day workings within a research environment.

BONUS POINTS	EDUCATION BS, geology, specialty in oceanography; MS, marine geology and geophysics	ON THE WEB National Oceanic and Atmospheric Administration (*www.noaa. gov*)	RELATED CAREERS physical limnologists, ocean engineer, marine lawyer, underwater acoustician, laboratory technician

Environmental Issues

VOLCANOLOGIST

Jeff Byrnes has studied lava flows and explosive eruptions in exotic locations such as Hawaii, Peru, and New Zealand. But his work does not stop here on Earth. As a planetary volcanologist, Byrnes uses his studies from Earth to develop an understanding of volcanic activity on Mars and Venus. A postdoctoral reseacher at the University of North Dakota, he strives to understand the phenomena of volcanism, predicting eruptions and alleviating volcanic hazards. Volcanologists foster scientific discovery as well as make predictions that can save lives.

WHAT INSPIRED YOU TO BECOME A VOLCANOLOGIST?

My route to becoming a volcanologist was rather circuitous. I was exposed to geology my junior year of college when I became an environmental geology major. Through undergraduate studies I developed skills in geomorphology [the study of landforms] and a general background in geology. I became interested in pursuing planetary geology while taking a planetary materials course my senior year, after which I attended a talk concerning lava flows on Mars at a professional conference. This sparked my interest, and I began my graduate studies in planetary volcanism [volcanic activity] the following fall. As part of my doctorate in geology, I studied volcanology and petrology; the geology of Mars, Venus, the Moon, and Io [a moon of Jupiter]; remote sensing and geographical information systems (GIS); and the history of the early Earth.

DESCRIBE YOUR WORK.

I study volcanic landforms to understand the processes by which they form in different planetary environments. I examine volcanoes on Earth using field and remote sensing analyses, which I then use as a basis for comparison with remote sensing analyses of volcanic features on other planetary bodies. For example, I extensively studied lava flows on Kilauea Volcano in Hawaii by making detailed field measurements and observations in conjunction with analyses of visible-, thermal-, and radar-wavelength image data acquired from airborne and spaceborne instruments. Then, I applied what I learned from Hawaiian volcanism to study lava flows on Venus and Io using NASA Magellan and Voyager data, respectively.

I enjoy my work for several reasons. Foremost I find volcanoes incredibly interesting and, as a field-oriented volcanologist, I enjoy traveling to see beautiful volcanoes around the world.

50

Additionally, I have the opportunity to experience various cultures of people living in volcanic areas. As a planetary scientist, comparing volcanoes on Earth with volcanoes on other planetary bodies allows me to explore other worlds through analysis of spacecraft data. Planetary studies also have developed my appreciation for the significance of volcanism as a process in the solar system and the incredible power associated with volcanic activity.

World travel is an enjoyable part of Jeff Byrnes's work.

ADVICE FOR STUDENTS?

To be a professional scientist researching volcanism, a doctorate in a related field such as geology or geophysics is normally required. Because volcanologists use a variety of different methods to study volcanism [such as petrology and geochemistry, physical and numerical modeling, geophysics and remote sensing, and mapping] many different skills and educational backgrounds are useful. It is essential to take science and math courses in high school. Good speaking, writing, and computer skills are important to conduct research and disseminate findings. Ultimately, the best way to appreciate volcanoes is to visit one.

DO YOU THINK WE WILL EVER PREDICT ERUPTIONS PERFECTLY?

Understanding of volcanic phenomena undoubtedly will continue to advance. However, I find it unlikely that it will ever progress to the point where we are able to perfectly predict when an eruption will start, what style of eruption will occur, where materials will be deposited, and how long it will last. In the future, I think that the number of volcanoes actively monitored will continue to increase and hazard mitigation efforts will continue to improve.

BONUS POINTS	EDUCATION	ON THE WEB	RELATED CAREERS
	BS, environmental geology; PhD, geology	Smithsonian Institution's Global Volcanism Program (*www.volcano.si.edu*); University of North Dakota's Volcano World (*www.volcanoworld.org*)	glacial geologist, paleontologist, park naturalist, soil scientist, astronomer

HURRICANE RESEARCHER

If you are curious about the forces of nature, you might enjoy the field of meteorology. Meteorologists work at understanding Earth's atmospheric phenomena and how they affect Earth and life on our planet. The phenomena could be global warming or, in Christopher Landsea's case, hurricanes. As a hurricane researcher with the Hurricane Research Division of the National Oceanic and Atmospheric Administration's (NOAA) Atlantic Oceanographic and Meteorological Laboratory (AOML), Landsea has flown into more than a dozen hurricanes. Although some may call this work dangerous, he calls it fun.

WHAT INSPIRED YOU TO BECOME A METEOROLOGIST?

While growing up in Miami, I witnessed seasonal storms with eyes during the summer and fall. As I listened to local weathermen refer to these storms by name, I found myself becoming interested in hurricanes. Consequently, I became involved in a wonderful program, Community Laboratory Research, during my senior year of high school. Two days a week I left school early to work with meteorologists Jack Parrish and Frank Marks at the NOAA/AOML/Hurricane Research Division. Once in a while after work, I would go windsurfing with Parrish across the street. I was hooked on meteorology. I thought, "Wow, work for a few hours and then go windsurfing. Being a weatherman is for me!" A couple of decades later, and here I am working at the same place I got my start. While it has turned out to be a bit more work than my experience back in high school, it still is hard to believe that I actually get paid a salary for such a fun profession.

WHAT SKILLS ARE NEEDED?

A good education is key to becoming a research meteorologist. In addition, working with a variety of people in the field helps pin down an area of interest to study. This work could be as a paid intern, but even an unpaid volunteer position is helpful to get a start. Researchers typically need a master's in science or a doctorate in meteorology. I have a bachelor's degree from the University of California at Los Angeles and a master's and doctorate from Colorado State University—all in atmospheric science. A strong undergraduate education background is required in mathematics, physics, and computers.

DESCRIBE YOUR WORK.

I don't make day-to-day forecasts of the storms. That is what the meteorologists at the National Hurricane Center do. And I can't say that I can actually do much about the hurricanes themselves, but I'm trying my best to understand why some years are busy, while some are very quiet. We utilize results from these studies to enhance our seasonal hurricane forecasts. I've also been involved with a project in recent years concerning a reassessment of historical hurricanes and fixing up, when needed, the tracks and intensities of storms in the database. We also occasionally discover tropical storms or hurricanes that no one had previously recognized in the past. We're currently busy revisiting the decades of the 1910s, 1920s, and 1930s.

During most of the year, I do quite a bit of computer analysis, write papers, attend meetings, and give talks. I certainly enjoy that part of it, but nothing beats what we do during the hurricane season—flying right into and through the storms themselves as part of our annual field program. Most hurricane flights may seem fairly boring to nonmeteorologists—10 hours of gray clouds in every direction, and no sensation of the winds swirling around the hurricane. But it definitely gets interesting when flying through the hurricane's rainbands [bands of showers characterized by strong gusty winds and heavy rains], which can get a bit turbulent, and the eyewall [a donutlike ring of thunderstorms that surround the calm eye]. Flying through the eyewall can be quite bouncy and exhilarating. But within the eye of a hurricane, like Andrew or Isabel, exists a place of powerful beauty. The most incredible sight is the middle of a strong hurricane. Sunshine streams into the windows of the plane from a perfect circle of blue sky directly above the plane, surrounding the plane on all sides is the blackness of the eyewall's thunderstorms, and directly below the plane peeking through a few low clouds lies a violent ocean with 18 m-high waves crashing into one another. The partial vacuum of the hurricane's eye is like nothing else on Earth. I would much rather experience a hurricane this way, from the safety of a plane, than from the ground hit by a hurricane's full fury.

Environmental Issues

ETHNOBOTANIST

According to *Plant Talk* (2007), approximately 270,000 species of plants exist on Earth. The number of known species—including trees, flowers, fruits, and herbs—increases almost daily as scientists make new discoveries. From indigenous cultures in Australia to urban communities in the United States and everywhere in between, plants are used in clothing, medicine, furniture, food, and symbolic and spiritual rituals. Ethnobotanists, such as Maria Fadiman, study this relationship between people [ethno] and plants [botany]. In the rain forests of Latin America and African Savannas, home to hundreds of thousands of plant species, Fadiman works to help people and plants live in harmony.

HOW DID YOU CHOOSE THIS FIELD?

I had always wanted to do conservation work, but I was initially intimidated by science and studied Latin American literature as an undergraduate. Then, during my junior year of college, I was introduced to the rain forest as an ecotourist station volunteer. After my initial fright of spiders, snakes, and scorpions I was dazzled by the green leaves, parrots, monkeys, and waterfalls. I realized that all the fascinating elements around me involved biology, botany, ecology, zoology, and hydrology. How could I not be interested in science after that insight? And, as I learned about the ecosystem, I realized that the people who were teaching me about the rain forest were also a part of it. So, in order to truly be a conservationist, I needed to look at the whole picture, which includes people.

DESCRIBE YOUR WORK.

In cultures all over the world, plants have myriad applications in food [vegetables and fruits], medicine [herbal remedies], clothing [cotton], furniture [wood], symbolism [pumpkins on Halloween], and spirituality [evergreens on Christmas]. Working in the rain forests of Latin America and African Savannas, I focus primarily on sustainability of plant resources.

To do this, I begin by interviewing indigenous peoples. I talk with healers, specialists, and interested villagers to understand how they gather and use plants. For instance, is a tree used for its bark, leaves, or fruit? Is the bark used for shelter or medicine? Villagers' practices may vary. When I learn of a plant resource collected and used in a sustainable way, I share that information with other villagers to encourage the approach. For example, I

54

worked with one group that cut down palm leaves for weaving with a special tool, which left the tree standing, while a different group cut down the entire tree for the same palm leaves. I conveyed knowledge about the former method to the latter group, providing an opportunity for more people to practice the sustainable technique.

Throughout my studies, I develop written records of the plant knowledge I gather. The records allow information, often lost through acculturation, to be accessed by future generations of indigenous peoples.

A TYPICAL DAY?

A typical day starts with the roosters beginning to call, long before the sun is up. I crawl out of my mosquito net, put on my rubber boots, and slip and slide down the muddy hill to the river where I brush my teeth. After a breakfast of rice and bananas, I go with villagers into the forest where they show me what plants they use and how. I spend the day interviewing villagers, cataloging the knowledge I have gathered, and selecting and collecting plants for cultivation and protection. I press and dry any plants I collect so that the specimens can be kept in an herbarium [a collection of preserved plant specimens for scientific study]. Before gathering with villagers around the fire for dinner, I walk off to the waterfall to take a quick rinse.

ADVICE FOR STUDENTS?

Ethnobotanists have degrees from a variety of fields, including archaeology, chemistry, ecology,

Fadiman with indigenous Lacandon children in Ciapas, Mexico, studying medicinal plants.

anthropology, linguistics, history, pharmacology, sociology, religion and mythology, botany, and ecology. After my first experience in a rain forest, I went on to obtain a master's degree that combined life sciences and anthropology. I then received a doctorate in geography, which is a field that merges the physical and human world.

In high school, students can start exploring ethnobotany by simply being aware of how plants are a part of daily life. Students could extend that everyday curiosity to investigate locally how Native Americans or early settlers used plants. Additionally, students might research the residents and plants of an unfamiliar location [such as a community in Australia or village in Africa]. It is helpful to read books by Mark Plotkin and Wade Davis, both of whom write in a fun and readable way about their ethnobotanical experiences. To get some hands-on experience, students can do volunteer work with environmental organizations.

AN EYE—OPENING EXPERIENCE?

I was working in Costa Rica with an indigenous group, the Guayami, and a woman spoke with me about her chronic stomach pain. She had been sick for years, and one day, the village was excited because they had obtained a doctor's appointment for her in a nearby town. She returned the next day thrilled to show me medicine she had obtained that would "cure" her. She opened her hands and there in a crumpled baggie was a handful of ibuprofen. I, of course, knew this would not cure her. Her sister turned to me and said "our father knew how to cure [stomach pain] with forest plants, but we don't know." In that moment, I realized how much knowledge is lost every day when a new generation does not learn the information held by previous generations.

BONUS POINTS	EDUCATION	ON THE WEB	RELATED CAREERS
	BS, Latin American literature; MS, Latin American studies; PhD, geography	An Introduction to Ethnobotany *(www. accessexcellence.org/RC/ Ethnobotany/page2.html)*; Society for Economic Botany *(www.econbot.org/ home.html)*	ethnopharmacologist, agronomist, botanist, food scientist, plant biotechnologist, landscape architect, anthropologist, ecologist, environmentalist

HEALTH AND FITNESS

DIABETES EDUCATOR

Our bodies need glucose (sugar) for energy. Sugar is transported through the body by way of the blood. Ideally, the pancreas releases the hormone *insulin* to take sugar from the blood into the cells. But what if the body does not produce or effectively use insulin? Sugar, with nowhere else to go, stays in the blood, and cells do not get fuel. As a result, blood sugar levels increase and diabetes is diagnosed. Diabetes can develop at any age and lead to a lot of health problems. But with the help of a diabetes educator—such as Donna Rice—individuals can learn the knowledge, skills, and tools needed to gain control of diabetes and have long, healthy lives.

WHAT IS DIABETES?

Diabetes is a disease in which the body does not make or correctly use insulin. There are three main types of this chronic condition. With Type 1 diabetes, usually diagnosed in children or young adults, the pancreas does not produce insulin. Type 2 diabetes develops when the body's cells ignore insulin or the pancreas does not produce enough insulin. Type 2 can develop at any age, and the chances of developing this most common form of diabetes are increased by obesity and inactivity. Some women develop gestational diabetes during pregnancy. This type of diabetes typically goes away after childbirth but increases the chances of a woman developing Type 2 later on in life.

DESCRIBE THIS JOB.

If left unmanaged, diabetes can lead to a slew of health problems in the kidneys, eyes, nerves, gums, teeth, and, most critically, the heart. This is where diabetes educators come in—we are professionals from various health-care fields who share in common education and training in the biological and social sciences, communication, counseling, education, and diabetes care. Diabetes educators deal with both the prevention and management of diabetes. We need an in-depth knowledge of science to assess, identify, and teach diabetes self-management goals, which vary by individual and diabetes type. Diabetes educators give patients a combination of science knowledge, coping mechanisms, and problem-solving tools to enable them to take charge, self-manage, and live well with diabetes. Patients learn about the diabetes disease process and how to prevent, detect, and treat complications through eating well, exercising, monitoring blood sugar, injecting insulin, and taking medication, for example.

58

ANY ADVICE FOR STUDENTS?

Diabetes is escalating at great speeds, and we do not have enough professionals in the area of diabetes care. The job market is wide open. Diabetes educators come from a range of backgrounds, including registered nurses, dietitians, pharmacists, and exercise physiologists. With this in mind, students are encouraged to pursue a post–high school education in any field of health care that interests them. To specialize in diabetes care, students should become familiar with the further academic, professional, and experiential criteria needed to become a certified diabetes educator (CDE). Meeting the additional care criteria to become a CDE is not required of diabetes educators, but it is encouraged.

HOW DID YOU CHOOSE THIS FIELD?

I have both a personal and a professional reason for becoming a diabetes educator. Personally, I have several family members who are dealing with diabetes. Professionally, I have a love for medicine and teaching, and I believe we can help fight the war on diabetes in the United States through healthy living. We have a lot of work to do in schools and in communities to increase the knowledge base around exercise and nutrition. I have a passion for nursing and education because I see great outcomes from my efforts. The challenges are considerable, but the rewards are even greater.

BONUS POINTS	EDUCATION RN, BS in nursing; MBA; CDE	ON THE WEB American Association of Diabetes Educators *(www. aadenet.org)*; American Diabetes Association *(www. diabetes.org)*	RELATED CAREERS nurse, physician, mental health professional, podiatrist, optometrist

GENETIC COUNSELOR

Providing information and support to families at risk for birth defects, genetic disorders, or inherited conditions, Jennifer Facher's job is twofold. She uses her scientific knowledge to help patients grasp complex medical concepts involving their genetic predispositions and provides emotional support as they make important health decisions. As a pediatric genetic counselor (GC) in the University Hospitals of Cleveland, Center for Human Genetics, Facher says that, to this day, the most satisfying part of her job is when patients thank her for playing a part in their ability to have healthy children.

WHAT INSPIRED YOU TO BECOME A GC?

In eleventh grade, I had a wonderful, down-to-earth biology teacher who invited a GC to speak with our class. The GC gave a fascinating presentation about genetic disorders and her role working with families affected by the disorders. Afterward I sat for hours in the library reading books on the subject. From then on I knew I wanted to become a GC someday.

WHAT DOES A GC DO?

There are various work settings for different types of GCs [such as prenatal, cancer, and pediatric]. Pediatric GCs typically work with physicians to evaluate children suspected to have a genetic syndrome due to birth defects, developmental difference, or physical differences not characteristic of the family. The counselor explains the suspicions, syndromes, and testing procedures to the family. After a diagnosis has been made, GCs discuss recurrence risks and what the diagnosis means for the affected individuals.

PLEASE DESCRIBE A TYPICAL DAY AT WORK.

On a clinic day, I am usually scheduled to see about six or seven patients. I begin by allowing a family to explain what they hope to gain from our visit and what they have discussed with their doctors. From this meeting, I learn the extent to which the family understands their child's disease. I then take complete medical, developmental, and family histories, and explain that the geneticist will conduct a physical examination of the child and discuss any genetic testing they feel is warranted. I present the histories to the geneticist, facilitate the testing process, report results, and arrange follow-ups.

Jennifer Facher decided in high school to become a genetic counselor.

WHAT EDUCATIONAL BACKGROUND AND SKILLS ARE NEEDED?

I tailored my college experience—with a bachelor's degree in biology—to meet the requirements for a master's program in genetic counseling. I went on to receive the master's from the University of Pittsburgh. Undergraduate degrees in nursing, psychology, and chemistry can also lead to careers in this field. Most GCs take a certification exam given by the American Board of Genetic Counselors to become board-certified genetic counselors. GCs need to be able to work well in a team environment [including with physicians,

nurses, and basic scientists] and in emotionally charged situations [such as with families contemplating continuing pregnancies affected with genetic disorders]. The GC approach is traditionally nondirective, meaning that while we provide families with accurate information about the disease, recurrence risks, and support options, we leave all medical decisions up to the family.

WHAT ADVICE WOULD YOU GIVE TO STUDENTS?

GCs not only discuss the science of genetics but also provide psychosocial support. GCs must know how to talk to people in a composed, friendly, and conversational manner to develop a good rapport with families and reduce their anxieties. Students should not only explore the science of genetics but also whether they are comfortable simply working with people going through difficult times. For example, volunteering at nursing homes, women's shelters, and hospitals are good opportunities to practice and develop conversational and listening skills. The National Society of Genetic Counselors website at *www.nsgc.org* provides information about this field.

BONUS POINTS	EDUCATION BS, biology; MS, genetic counseling	ON THE WEB National Society of Genetic Counselors (*www.nsgc.org)*	RELATED CAREERS registered nurse, physician, psychologist, occupational therapist, social worker

RADIATION THERAPIST

Cancer encompasses more than 125 diseases. In the United States alone, more than 1 million people will be diagnosed with cancer this year. Approximately 70% of cancer patients will receive radiation therapy. The goal of radiation therapy is to eradicate cancer cells while sparing normal cells. Because radiation therapy is such an important part of treating cancer, there is a growing need in all parts of the world for competent, excellent, and caring radiation therapists like Robert Adams, the program director of Radiation Therapy for the University of North Carolina Hospitals.

WHAT INSPIRED YOU TO BECOME A RADIATION THERAPIST?

My career as a radiation therapist is directly linked to my mom's dying of ovarian cancer during my junior year of college. She was diagnosed with cancer when I was a college freshman. As I accompanied her during cancer treatments, I learned about the various people who worked with cancer patients. Although I was originally a history major, I came to realize my life's work would be working with and caring for cancer patients. From this personal experience, I chose a career in radiation therapy.

DESCRIBE YOUR WORK.

A radiation therapist is a valuable member of a cancer treatment team who delivers radiation treatments to patients, helps construct treatment plans, and works with cancer patients and their families. In a typical day, four patients are treated per hour. A patient treated with radiation therapy can receive only a limited amount of radiation dose each day. Consequently, it takes anywhere from two to eight weeks to complete a treatment regimen. The radiation therapist works with a patient every day of the patient's radiation treatment. Radiation therapists must plan, evaluate, and assess several parameters for each patient every day.

WHAT BACKGROUND IS NEEDED?

An individual can become a radiation therapist through two avenues: completing a two- or four-year radiologic technology program and then attending a one-year radiation therapy program, or achieving a four-year baccalaureate degree in

62

radiation therapy. I have an undergraduate degree in radiologic science with health-care certifications in medical imaging, radiation therapy, and medical dosimetry. I also have a master's degree in health policy and administration and a doctorate in higher education administration.

Robert Adams became a radiation therapist because he wanted to care for cancer patients.

ANY ADVICE FOR STUDENTS?

A student interested in radiation therapy should contact the guidance counselor and community radiation therapy or radiology department about programs in the region. The professional organization for radiation therapists is the American Society of Radiologic Technologists (*asrt.org*); the certifying agency for radiation therapists is the American Registry of Radiologic Technologists (*http://arrt.org*); and the accrediting agency for radiation therapy school programs is the Joint Review Committee for Radiologic Technology (*http://jrcert.org*). If all else fails, please feel free to contact me at *robert_adams@med.unc.edu*. I have helped many students with health-care careers.

Currently, I give talks to several local high schools. Not only do I talk about radiation therapy, but I also discuss how the use of radiation can benefit humans and improve the quality of our lives through both medical imaging and radiation therapy.

WHAT IS THE MOST REWARDING ASPECT OF YOUR CAREER?

First, seeing and speaking with patients whom I treated 10 to 15 years ago and having them give me a hug is very rewarding. Second, as a radiation therapy teacher I see the accomplishments of our program's alumni and the many lives they have touched and the people they have cared for and helped cure. We are very proud of each graduate. Their work is noble and greatly benefits humanity.

BONUS POINTS	EDUCATION	ON THE WEB	RELATED CAREERS
	BS, radiologic science; MPH, health policy and administration; EdD, higher education administration; registered radiation therapist (RT); certified medical dosimetrist (CMD)	American Registry of Radiologic Technologists (*arrt.org*); American Society of Radiologic Technologists (*asrt.org*); Joint Review Committee for Radiologic Technology (*jrcert.org*)	radiation oncologist, medical physicist, dosimetrist, oncology nurse, medical assistant, medical laboratory technologist, veterinarian

Health and Fitness

RESPIRATORY THERAPIST

Whether treating newborns for breathing disorders, helping patients with asthma, or diagnosing sleep disorders, respiratory therapists help people breathe easier. Treating and diagnosing lung disease requires a strong reserve of scientific knowledge. Today, as president of the American Association for Respiratory Care, respiratory therapist John D. Hiser is passionate about his role in getting people the care they need. When Hiser was in high school, though, he did not know what he wanted to be when he grew up. In fact, in 1966, he went to college intent on becoming an accountant. But a twist of fate landed Hiser in the Navy and consequently launched a lifelong career of helping patients and saving lives.

DESCRIBE THIS FIELD.

Respiratory care has an array of different specialties to suit individual interests and goals. For example, neonatal respiratory therapists (RTs) work in children's hospitals and treat newborns for breathing disorders. Pulmonary RTs educate and treat patients with chronic lung diseases such as asthma and chronic bronchitis. Critical care RTs are drawn to the fast pace of the intensive care unit and work with the most technical equipment and severely ill patients.

RTs also work outside of hospitals. In the back of helicopters and ambulances, transport RTs work closely with nurses, physicians, and emergency medical technicians to stabilize patients until they reach a hospital. RTs who work in polysomnography—sleep medicine technology—must understand the 77 identified sleep disorders and usually work in sleep laboratories during the night shift when studies are conducted. Some RTs make home visits to provide services to patients with long-term illnesses like emphysema. These career paths, to name a few, are just some of the many available to RTs.

Depending on his or her area of expertise, an RT might diagnose lung disorders and recommend treatment methods; analyze breath, tissue, and blood specimens for oxygen levels; or monitor and maintain mechanical ventilation and artificial airway devices. All RTs in all specialties need a strong education and solid training in science and technology.

WHAT BACKGROUND IS NEEDED?

An RT must have a strong background in anatomy, physiology, chemistry, physics, microbiology, pharmacology, and medical terminology. All of these areas provide essential knowledge that is used on a daily basis when treating or diagnosing lung disease. Individuals are required to complete either a two-year associate's degree or a four-year bachelor's degree. Graduates from these programs are eligible to take two levels of national licensing exams. Passing the entry-level exam leads to a Certified Respiratory Therapist (CRT) credential. Subsequently, passing an additional, advanced two-part exam leads to a Registered Respiratory Therapist (RRT) credential.

HOW DID YOU BECOME AN RT?

I didn't really choose my career; it chose me. In high school, my focus was less on a future profession and more on whether or not I would be going to Vietnam. I went to college and planned to major in accounting, but I had to drop out due to financial issues. I was immediately drafted, joined the Navy instead of the Army, and was sent off to boot camp. Upon my return from boot camp, I decided to become a hospital corpsman—a cross between a nurse and a paramedic. I spent a year taking care

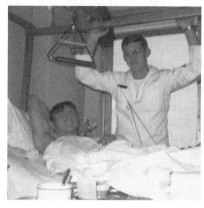

As a Navy hospital corpsman, John Hiser took care of returnees from Vietnam.

of Vietnam returnees in the orthopedic ward of a Naval hospital. One day the head nurse told me she was transferring me to the inhalation therapy [respiratory therapy] unit. I told her that I did not think I could "put tubes down people's throats," but she believed I could and the next day I started my on-the-job training [training in respiratory therapy, pulmonary function testing, assisting anesthesiologists with surgeries, and acting as a recovery room nurse].

Once I was a fully trained senior corpsman, I was transferred to Vietnam where I spent a year on a destroyer escort responsible for picking up downed pilots in a rescue boat; served on the gun line [bombing targets]; and spent a month serving on a spy ship. Once I was discharged, I came home to Fort Worth and went to Tarrant County Junior College [now Tarrant County College, Texas] to get my associate's in applied science in respiratory care. I continued to pursue training and education in respiratory therapy; today I am the director of that same program and have taught at Tarrant County for 28 years.

Today Hiser teaches others in the field of respiratory therapy.

Professionally, the Navy and the fact that someone else picked my career was the best thing that ever happened to me. I love what I do. And still, the most rewarding experiences I have had with patients involved taking care of the marines and sailors returning from Vietnam. Their positive attitudes were amazing in the face of what they had endured.

BONUS POINTS	EDUCATION	ON THE WEB	RELATED CAREERS
	Hospital corpsman; AAS, respiratory therapy; BS, allied health education; MEd., vocational education/secondary higher education; CRT; RRT; respiratory care practitioner (RCP); certified pulmonary function technologist (CPFT)	National Board for Respiratory Care (*www. nbrc.org*); American Association for Respiratory Care (*www.aarc.org*)	radiation oncologist, medical physicist, dosimetrist, oncology nurse, medical assistant, medical laboratory technologist, veterinarian

Health and Fitness

SPORT BIOMECHANIST

If you are an athlete or sports enthusiast, you know every second counts. To find that 1% to 2% improvement that can make the difference between 1st and 5th place, sport biomechanists use science to investigate sports techniques and equipment, seeking ways to improve performance and reduce injury risk. In essence, they want athletes to train smarter, not harder. At the U.S. Olympic Training Center, Colorado Springs, Colorado, Bill Sands is the head of Sport Biomechanics and Engineering, which is responsible for the service and research needs of 45 sports. Helping Olympic athletes defeat their opponents and achieve their dreams is a high-pressure job, but Sands steps up to the plate with his lifelong passion for science and sport.

DESCRIBE A SPORT BIOMECHANIST'S JOB.

We help sports in two basic ways; both involve science. The first is service, which consists of analyzing coach and athlete needs, implementing relevant tests to determine athlete status, interpreting this information, and reporting back to coaches and athletes. This service allows athletes to modify training and enhance performance, but cutting-edge investigations are needed to really push a sport forward. Therefore, the second element in our job is applied research and innovation, which involves conducting experiments on various aspects of training such as technique, conditioning, and technology.

Finding ways to improve performance requires applying the principles of kinematics [movement] and kinetics [forces]. We use a diverse array of technologies—such as video motion software, sensing and timing equipment, and electromyography—to record subtle measurements and analyze performance. In addition to our research, coaches and athletes often tend to jump on "new," untested methods or technologies, which range from good luck charms to ineffective nutritional supplements. Using science, an impartial and effective means of assessing methods and claims, we have to determine if the new approaches actually work.

HOW DID YOU CHOOSE THIS FIELD?

Growing up as a gymnast, I tried my hardest to be an Olympian, looking to science to understand and improve my own performance. As an

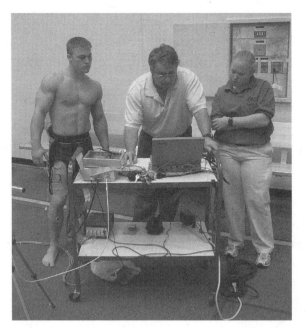

Bill Sands (center) helps future Olympians improve their performances.

of artificial intelligence techniques in monitoring athlete training.

After coaching gymnastics for several years, I went on to graduate school. Sport biomechanics was not offered as a concentration at the school I attended, so I obtained a degree in exercise physiology while focusing my research on mechanically oriented experiments on athletes. My positions after graduate school included director of research and development for USA Gymnastics and senior sports physiologist for the U.S. Olympic Committee (USOC).

WHAT BACKGROUND IS NEEDED?

Individuals interested in applied sport science should concentrate first on a basic science education. A sports background is also extremely useful. My major asset in working with athletes and coaches is the fact that I have been an athlete and high-level coach myself.

undergraduate, I took most of the typical math and science courses—biology, physiology, and chemistry—but focused on subjects that would lead to applied sport science. Also, my college gymnastics coach was very devoted to science and applied biomechanical principles in our training. In many ways, gymnastics is an excellent laboratory for the study of physics.

Hoping to help fulfill someone else's Olympic dreams, I turned to coaching after college, constantly seeking new ways to apply science through exercise physiology and biomechanics. Before computer technology was a common instrument used in assessing athlete performance, for instance, I taught myself computer programming and developed a two-dimensional kinematic analysis system. I also explored the use

Moreover, a sports background allows me to understand the no-nonsense outlook of coaches and athletes, who are unwilling to be guinea pigs when the possibility of a payoff seems remote. A good deal of "sales" and interpretation of data is needed to persuade coaches and athletes that your investigations are worth their time. Without some very sound reasoning, it is difficult to convince a celebrity athlete that participation in an investigation is going to increase his or her chances of winning a medal. Most high-level athletes believe that, if it is not busted, do not fix it. When athletes are at the top of their game, essentially they are not busted.

ADVICE FOR STUDENTS?

Even in high school, students can begin studying sport science [with the help of a coach or teacher]. Athletes should keep training logs on everything they do from laps and weights to sleep quality and nutrition. These logs provide abundant data that can be analyzed in countless ways. Students can also record track-and-field races and analyze the performances by tracing the athlete frame by frame from video using overhead projector acetate sheets or simple video-editing programs. With a heart rate monitor, students can study metabolic responses to all aspects of training. Students should record injuries and study potential mechanisms— self-reported data [such as feelings and sleep patterns] are very handy for studying and preventing overtraining and injuries.

Students can also attend conferences on sport and exercise science or take classes from a local university with an athletic, sport, or exercise science program. I should draw a distinction between exercise science and sport science. When looking into higher education, students should be sure to determine the emphasis of the particular program. While many university programs prepare exercise scientists, sport science programs are relatively uncommon. Exercise scientists are fond of using athletes to demonstrate something in biology and mechanics, but the direct study of athletes for the sake of enhancing their performance has become quite rare.

Once undergraduate school is completed, the USOC offers internships for students, allowing them to live at an Olympic training center and work closely with many sports. The positions are competitive, but they offer aspiring sport scientists the opportunity to work alongside Olympic athletes and established scientists.

BONUS POINTS	EDUCATION BS; MS and PhD, exercise physiology	ON THE WEB U.S. Olympic Internship Program (www.usoc.org/12675.htm); Exploratorium's Sport Science Exhibit (www.exploratorium.edu/sports)	RELATED CAREERS sport physiologist, sport psychologist, personal trainer, coach, nutritionist, physical therapist, cardiac rehabilitation specialist, occupational therapist, sport physician

Health and Fitness

EAR, NOSE, AND THROAT DOCTOR

Ear, nose, and throat complaints—such as allergies, ear infections, sinusitis, and sore throats—are the number one reason people go to the doctor. Diseases and disorders of the head and neck, particularly the ear, nose, and throat (ENT), are treated by ENT physicians. Although the field is limited to the head and neck, it is a very important area of the body and the location of all the special senses [sight, hearing, smell, and taste]. Using investigative thinking, ENT doctor Scott Howard helps his diverse group of patients with medicine, lifestyle alterations, therapies, and surgery.

WHAT DO ENT DOCTORS TREAT?

Our branch of medicine is called *otolaryngology*—head and neck surgery. Otolaryngology [short for otorhinolaryngology] is derived from the root words *otos* [ear], *rhino* [nose], and *laryngo* [windpipe]. An otolaryngologist, therefore, is literally someone who studies the ear, nose, and throat, which is why we are most commonly known as ENT doctors.

Because our training is in both medicine and surgery, we diagnose, treat, and manage head and neck diseases and disorders. This means we see patients with primary care and clinical problems and, rather than refer them to other specialists, also perform surgical procedures. We help people with problems related to the sinuses [such as nose bleeds, stuffy nose], larynx [such as sore throat, reflux disease], and ears [such as infections, hearing loss]. We also treat cancer in the head and neck [such as neck, nose, ear, skull base], conduct plastic and reconstructive surgery on the face and neck [such as protruding ears, rhinoplasty], and manage allergies [such as hay fever].

PLEASE DESCRIBE A TYPICAL DAY AT WORK.

I am a fourth-year resident at Walter Reed Army Medical Center, in Washington, DC. Every morning for about an hour I conduct "rounds" on patients admitted to the hospital. In other words, I check on inpatients and perform physical exams, which entail looking at vital signs, lab values, and test results. I discuss findings with patients, their families, and nurses and order additional tests if necessary. The rest of the day is either spent in the clinic, seeing a diverse group of patients with equally diverse ENT problems, or in surgery. On operating days, I perform procedures such as sinus operations, tonsillectomies, ear tube insertions, and extensive surgeries for head and neck cancer or advanced ear disease. At the end of the day, I round again to check on my inpatients. I am also on call from home one to two nights per week, which requires responding by phone or in person to any emergencies or patient questions. For example, I am frequently called in emergency situations to evaluate a patient's airway or upper digestive tract.

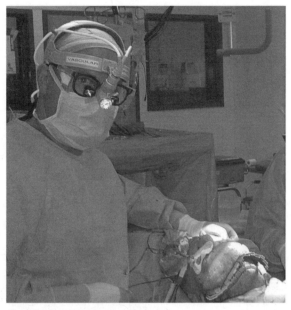

Scott Howard in the operating room.

ADVICE FOR STUDENTS?

Training includes a four-year undergraduate degree, four years of medical school, a one-year surgical internship, and four additional years of ENT residency. At the conclusion of the residency, many surgeons complete a fellowship. A fellowship is a one- or two- year specialized period of training in a field such as facial plastic surgery, rhinology [nose and sinus surgery], otology [ear and base of skull surgery], laryngology [voice and throat disorders], or head and neck surgery [treating cancers of the head and neck]. To learn more about the field, students should contact their local ENT physician to arrange a lunch visit on a clinic day.

WHAT IS YOUR BACKGROUND?

In high school, I enjoyed and excelled in math and science—I actually recall my 10th-grade biology teacher telling me I might be a good doctor. After high school I went to West Point where I obtained a bachelor's degree in aerospace engineering. I then spent the following five years in the Army serving as an Armor Officer in the 1st Cavalry Division at Fort Hood, Texas. During that time, I was considering going back to school for a master's degree in biomedical engineering. However, I had always enjoyed helping people and wanted to learn more about medicine, so on Friday nights I volunteered at the Darnall Army Community Hospital. One emergency room doctor thought I had an aptitude for medicine and recommended I consider medical school. I realized that was exactly what I wanted to do.

I attended the University of Pennsylvania for a year and a half to take additional courses [such as organic chemistry and biology] required for medical school admission. After preparing for the Medical College Admissions Test (MCAT) and achieving a high score, I went on to medical school at the University of Florida.

A MEMORABLE EXPERIENCE?

Some patients come to me complaining of a sore throat or a lump in their neck and I discover an early form of cancer, sometimes caused by smoking or drinking alcohol. This is a very sad moment for me and the patient, but it is also a moment where I am able to provide information and an elaborate treatment plan that will give them a fighting chance. Although a cure is not always possible, I know that being there for patients in this time of need is of great value.

	EDUCATION	ON THE WEB	RELATED CAREERS
BONUS POINTS	BS, aerospace engineering; MD	The American Academy of Otolaryngology–Head and Neck Surgery *(www.entnet. org)*	nurse, dentist, surgical technologist, physician's assistant, physical therapist, orthotics and prosthetics practitioner, audiologist, speech-language pathologist

Health and Fitness

CLINICAL NEUROPSYCHOLOGIST

Neuroscience is a field dedicated to learning about the brain and nervous system, which can help us understand, prevent, and treat diseases and disorders such as Alzheimer's, depression, and addiction. The vast scope of questions neuroscience is trying to answer draws interest from many disciplines, including psychology. Clinical neuropsychologists, such as Deborah Attix, help people who appear to have cognitive or behavioral problems. Using scientific tests to assess what parts of the brain might be linked to certain problems, Attix gets an overall picture of someone's cognitive function. With this information, she can diagnose a disorder and provide targeted treatment to help that person recover or cope.

DESCRIBE THIS FIELD.

Clinical neuropsychologists are psychologists who specialize in assessment and treatment of memory and behavior in relationship to central nervous system functioning. Assessment includes an array of objective paper-and-pencil, computerized, and interview-style psychological tests, which measure behavior, memory, and thinking skills known to be linked to particular brain structures or pathways. These tests evaluate whether or not someone is having cognitive problems, the affected area [such as memory, language, attention, visual-spatial analysis], and the severity of the deficits. Factors shown to affect performance, such as age and educational background, are taken into account. The test results are not definitive but rather are

tools that give us an overall picture of someone's cognitive function. Based on the findings, we make diagnostic inferences about what systems of the brain might be affected and what illnesses might be operating. With a diagnosis, we recommend treatment that can help people recover from or adapt to their dysfunction.

A TYPICAL DAY?

A typical day at work involves patient evaluations, feedback, intervention, research, and teaching. Evaluations are done by a team and can take several hours. Patients are often referred by other physicians, so we begin by reviewing medical information to determine the reason for referral, such as differentiating between depression

Deborah Attix works on bad brains.

and neurologically based memory problems or identifying if the patient has a cortically based memory disorder [such as Alzheimer's disease]. We then interview the patient to determine relevant medical history, including symptom onset, the course of the illness, and its effects on functioning. Next, a psychometrician [data technician] administers and scores neuropsychological tests, which I later interpret. These tests look at skills such as the patient's memory, higher-level reasoning, sequencing, language, visual-spatial, and fine motor; mood; and attention.

While the psychometrician administers tests, I might give another patient feedback from an examination or provide intervention sessions. Interventions are designed to help people compensate for and adjust to the changes they experience as a result of their diagnosis. For some patients, this involves cognitive training—such as targeting improvement of memory and

processing skills—while for others intervention entails psychotherapy. In addition to helping patients, I also work with clinical research teams on cognitive aspects of studies and teach clinical neuropsychology graduate students, interns, and postdoctoral fellows.

ADVICE FOR STUDENTS?

The education required is a bachelor's degree, typically in psychology, followed by a doctorate in clinical psychology with a neuroscience focus [such as courses in neuroanatomy and neurobiology]. Essential specialty training in clinical neuropsychology occurs during the predoctoral internship and postdoctoral fellowship. Because a fellowship is usually a two-year training experience, the entire journey from high school to independent practice takes approximately 10 years. Students should not be discouraged— many occupations require extensive study and preparation [such as physicians, attorneys, scientific researchers]. Further, the journey is typically fascinating and rewarding. Students also should note that neuroscience in general is an exciting and continually evolving field. There are many career opportunities in allied disciplines, including education, basic research, neuroimaging, and even computer science.

High school students interested in learning more should shadow a clinical neuropsychologist in their community and become familiar with various practice arenas. From private practice to major medical centers, there is considerable variance in focus, clinical work, research, and teaching. Interested students can also learn a lot online and by reading some basic neuropsychology texts, such as Lezak's *Neuropsychological Assessment* or Kolb and Wishaw's *Fundamentals of Clinical Neuropsychology.*

WHY DO YOU LIKE YOUR CAREER?

In my first year of graduate school, I took a class in the biological bases of behavior and was fascinated. Almost 20 years later, I find myself still captivated and excited about my field. Many specialty areas of practice in medicine have a well-defined system for evaluation and treatment. The brain, however, is amazing in its complexity and our knowledge remains in its infancy despite constant progress. There is always new research and new understanding, and there are always more questions. It is a field that will keep one challenged, learning, and humble. The opportunity to participate in the rewarding process of moving forward is immense and a privilege, both at the level of the individual patient and the level of the field.

	EDUCATION	ON THE WEB	RELATED CAREERS
BONUS POINTS	BS, psychology; PhD, clinical psychology	American Psychological Association's Division of Clinical Neuropsychology *(www.div40.org)*	psychiatrist, neurologist, neurological surgeon, psychometrician, neurochemist, electroneurodiagnostic technician, artificial intelligence expert

LET'S INVESTIGATE

CRYPTOGRAPHER

For the general public, cryptography became well known as the method used to uncover secrets in Dan Brown's fictional bestseller *The Da Vinci Code*. But the science of cryptography has been popular for centuries—hieroglyphics discovered in Egypt suggest that code making dates back almost 4,000 years.

In today's society, cryptographers like Bruce Schneier provide security systems for computers and networks. When an item is purchased over the internet, for instance, cryptography is applied to encrypt credit-card numbers so that the information cannot be detected by hackers. Government agencies use the science to send messages around the world safely. Schneier has designed and broken encryption algorithms and cryptographic systems for hundreds of commercial products and companies.

DESCRIBE YOUR FIELD.

Traditionally, cryptography is used to send secret messages between two points. A sender uses a key to transform an original message into a code [encryption] and a receiver must use that same key to break the code [decryption]. During wartime, particularly World War II, cryptographers designed codes to encrypt and decrypt confidential text messages. But with the rise of computers and the internet, cryptography has become so much more. Modern methods of cryptography use mathematics and computer programming, with keys based on complicated algorithms, to design and analyze mathematical security systems. In addition to secrecy, cryptography provides authentication, data integrity, fairness, and a whole slew of other security solutions.

A cryptologist might work as a professor in a university, a consultant for a large company, or for the government [for example, the National Security Agency]. I have done most of my cryptography work as a consultant. I have designed and analyzed security systems for internet commerce, computer games, electronic gambling, e-mail, electronic voting, the authentication of digital images, web surfing, electronic identity cards, and fax machines. I have also done some work for the government.

WHAT BACKGROUND IS NEEDED?

Cryptography is just about the most fun that one can possibly have with mathematics, and, in addition, it touches some of the most basic and important problems involving the internet and society. It is always different, and it's always interesting. And, unlike other sciences, cryptography is inherently combative. One person invents something and someone else breaks it; and vice versa. There are few things more exciting than being the first to break someone else's cryptographic system. Conversely, we've all learned not to take it personally when someone else breaks our stuff.

To compete in this field, strong experience with mathematics, computer science, and scientific thinking are needed. Most cryptographers have undergraduate degrees in mathematics or computer science. Work can lean toward theoretical cryptography, which primarily uses math skills, or applied cryptography, in which programming skills are also important. Investigative techniques learned in science courses are often employed, such as when deciphering a code. Along the same lines, scientific thinking is always essential, including analyzing and interpreting data, experimental design, numerical computation, advanced quantitative skills, critical thinking, problem solving, logical thinking, and evaluating theoretical models.

ADVICE FOR STUDENTS?

Read. Great books include David Kahn's *The Codebreakers* [an absolute must for a historical perspective], and for students starting out, my books *Applied Cryptography* and *Secrets and Lies* are helpful. It is OK not to understand everything at first.

Start thinking like a security person. The security person looks at everything as a system and figures out how to break it. Students can investigate the security of things around their homes [computer programs or burglar alarms, for example] and consider how to break the security and then how to improve it. Everything has security, and it can all be analyzed, broken, and improved.

	EDUCATION	ON THE WEB	RELATED CAREERS
BONUS POINTS	BS, physics; MS, computer science	International Association for Cryptologic Research *(www.iacr.org)*; National Security Agency *(www.nsa.gov)*	artificial intelligence programmer, mathematician, software development specialist, systems analyst, security engineer

Let's Investigate

FORENSICS SERVICES TECHNICIAN

The popularity of television shows such as CBS's hit *CSI* and Discovery Channel's *The New Detectives* demonstrates how forensic science is capturing the attention of many people. But beyond entertainment, forensics play a crucial role in criminal investigation. Whether collecting evidence at a crime scene, processing evidence in the lab, or testifying in court, forensic services technicians (FSTs) unveil clues that criminals are not even aware they left behind. For Jason Birchfield, forensics supervisor of the Baltimore County Police Department Crime Scene Unit, science is an indispensable resource.

HOW DID YOU BECOME AN FST?

I really did not get interested in the field of forensics until after high school. In college, I took a variety of classes in an attempt to find a subject that sparked my interest. An introductory criminal justice course did just that. I clearly recall the first time I observed a fingerprint brush during an instructor demonstration. Although I had an interest in the field of criminal justice, I did not aspire to be a police officer. At this crossroad, I sought advice—the undisputed counsel was "go to school for something of interest and you will succeed." After receiving a bachelor's degree in criminal justice I became a private investigator, gained some field experience, and eventually attained a position with the police department as an FST. After three years I was promoted to my current position as supervisor.

WHAT DOES AN FST DO?

We are responsible for identifying, collecting, and preserving evidence at crime scene investigations in support of law enforcement activities. Photographing crime and accident scenes— including burglaries, robberies, deaths, autopsies, and assault victims—is necessary to record the appearance of evidence. FSTs also identify, collect, and secure physical evidence, such as blood, body fluids, hair, fibers, firearms, and narcotics, for laboratory testing and use as evidence in criminal prosecutions. We search for and develop fingerprints at crime scenes and participate in laboratory processing, as well as photograph and fingerprint suspects and victims. Other responsibilities include producing castings of footprints, tire tracks, and other impressions; preparing court presentations of evidence; and testifying in court.

WHAT TYPE OF FORENSIC EVIDENCE DO YOU RELY ON?

Fingerprints obtained in criminal investigations have long been considered one of the most valuable types of physical evidence that can be found at a crime scene. There are three different types of fingerprints: visible, impression, and latent. While visible prints can be photographed directly, and impression prints can be photographed under special lighting conditions, latent prints must first be made visible. Latent fingerprints are composed of several chemicals exuded through fingertip pores and are left on virtually every object touched. To retrieve these latent prints, we collect evidence from a crime scene, bring it to the lab, and process it using different techniques and substances, such as cyanoacrylate [super glue fumes], ninhydrin, fingerprint powder, magnetic powder, chemical dye stains, and digital photography. After the prints are recovered through those methods, digital images are taken and enhanced. Prints are then examined.

Jason Birchfield relies on science for his forensics work.

Once the unique characteristics are identified, the prints are imported into the Automated Fingerprint Identification System database to search for possible hits. No two people have the same fingerprints. We clear more crime using prints than any other type of forensic evidence.

WHAT BACKGROUND IS NEEDED?

The minimum educational background required for an FST is a bachelor's degree in a subject such as criminal justice, criminalistics, law enforcement, biology, or chemistry. However, employers also weigh field experience. Students should know that a complete background investigation is conducted upon application.

BONUS POINTS	EDUCATION	ON THE WEB	RELATED CAREERS
	BS, criminal justice	American Academy of Forensic Sciences (*www.aafs.org*); International Association for Identification (*www.theiai.org*)	medical examiner, police officer, crime laboratory analyst, forensic toxicologist, psychological profiler

Let's Investigate

BOMB INVESTIGATOR

When there is a bomb threat, bomb investigators come to the rescue. Bomb technicians and investigators use scientific techniques to get to the bottom of an incident. Barney T. Villa has served on the Los Angeles County Arson Explosives Detail for 18 years. Now, also the international director of the International Association of Bomb Technicians and Investigators, Villa continues to be motivated by the challenge of his profession—protecting lives and communities. Here, Villa gives us a peek into what makes his job tick.

WHAT DOES A BOMB INVESTIGATOR DO?

As bomb technicians and investigators for the L.A. County AED, we not only render an improvised explosive device [bomb] safe, we investigate the crime to apprehend the person responsible. Generally, our unit handles anywhere from 300 to 600 bomb investigations per year. When not responding to bomb calls, we conduct arson investigations to find the cause and origin of fires. In this line of work, safety measures—such as robots, x-ray machines, explosive-detecting K-9s, and teamwork—are essential. Two or more bomb technicians respond to a scene; one will generally wear a 32 kg bomb suit while the other assists with equipment preparation. The number one rule is to always respect the person you are working with and the device you are working on. Remaining in good physical shape and having a clear mind is paramount to our survival.

HOW IS SCIENTIFIC THINKING INVOLVED?

The process of investigation begins when we respond to a call. If an explosion or fire has occurred, the scene is photographed, witnesses are interviewed, and evidence is collected. This evidence [such as glass, metal fragments, charred wood, accelerant residue, and latent fingerprints] is documented, photographed, and subjected to hair and fiber exams; DNA, fingerprint, and materials analysis; and explosive residue and accelerant examinations. Examiners frequently conduct explosive tests to determine the overall design and function of devices—the design characteristics, materials, and details of the bomb's construction are a bomber's signature for a particular incident and aid in identifying a bomber. Records of convicted and suspect bombers and arsonists are maintained to determine links between incidents. The abilities to apply logic

82

and reasoning to identify possible solutions to an investigation, find relationships among seemingly unrelated events, and analyze data and information are very useful qualities.

WHAT BACKGROUND IS NEEDED?

Our team receives extensive training and basic information at the Hazardous Device School in Redstone Arsenal, Alabama. The main requirement in our unit is detective bureau experience, which prepares individuals with skills such as critical thinking, gathering evidence, questioning witnesses, judgment and decision making, and inductive reasoning. Education varies with each investigator. A former military person with explosive ordnance disposal expertise is a highly valuable candidate but must first become a police officer. My experience consists of 15 years as a deputy sheriff before joining the bomb squad, serving with the United States Marine Corps, obtaining an associate in arts degree, and, more recently, completing an occupational studies program. It is important for any high school student considering a job in law enforcement to stay out of jail and trouble with peers involved in illegal activities. For more

Bomb investigators use explosive-detecting dogs in their searches.

information about careers, students should visit the Law Enforcement Exploring website at *www. learning-for-life.org/exploring/lawenforcement.*

WHAT IS YOUR BIGGEST ACCOMPLISHMENT?

I work with the very best in our field, and to have survived all these years without injury is a major accomplishment. Also, our unit prepared an inspirational video presentation titled *Youth and Explosives*—a message from a 19-year-old boy who almost killed himself while experimenting with explosives. The peer-to-peer message in the video is a very effective medium to communicate the danger of explosives.

BONUS POINTS	EDUCATION	ON THE WEB	RELATED CAREERS
	United States Marine Corps; AA; BS, occupational studies	Law Enforcement Exploring (*www.learning-for-life.org/ exploring/lawenforcement*)	Federal Bureau of Investigation (FBI) agent, Secret Service agent, forensics technician, police officer

Let's Investigate

HISTORICAL ARCHAEOLOGIST

Historical archaeologists like Mark Warner, an associate professor of anthropology at the University of Idaho, investigate through excavations and written records how people lived in the recent past. History is considered recent rather than prehistoric when written sources from a period are available. If we already have documentary evidence, then why do we need to dig? In recent history, because only a relatively small percentage of the population made efforts to record the events of the day, the lives of many were never documented. For example, we know a lot about how someone like Thomas Jefferson lived because he wrote a great deal, but we know much less about other members of his family or about his slaves. Excavation of artifacts, in combination with written documents, has been able to tell archaeologists stories about how everyday individuals—like you and me—lived in the past.

DESCRIBE THIS FIELD.

Historical archaeology is quintessentially a social science—we study the relationships between historical objects and texts to discover information about human society. When we conduct an excavation, it is a team endeavor: Some members examine documents in local archives, some use transits to map out the excavation site, and still others excavate and process artifacts. After the digging is over, we head to the laboratory where the real work begins. In the lab, the identification, cataloging, analysis, conservation, and curation of artifacts occurs. This technical work gives us a full record of the dig and all of the objects we

recovered. The ultimate goal is to tell a story about how people lived in the past through the artifacts recovered in our excavations.

The basic objective in the lab is to make sure that artifacts do not suffer further damage or decay. In many cases, this is largely a matter of cleaning and storing the objects in chemically stable bags or boxes. Ceramics and glass generally require relatively little in the way of conservation. In contrast, bone and metal preservation can be more labor intensive. A consolidant is applied to arrest deterioration in particularly fragile bones, metal corrosion must be removed through sand blasting or electrolysis, and further corrosion is prevented

84

by a sealant application. In addition to conservation, we determine fragment counts for ceramics and glass, reconstruct broken shards to identify an object's function, and calculate weight estimates based on recovered bones.

WHAT IS A TYPICAL DAY LIKE?

For the past eight years, one of my projects has involved working with the Miami tribe of Oklahoma. The Miami Indians were forcibly moved by the U.S. government twice during the 19th century from their ancestral territories in Indiana and Ohio to Kansas and again to Oklahoma. For 15 years, the tribe has been trying to rediscover the history they lost through those relocations. My excavations in Oklahoma, as well as other archaeologists' work in Indiana, have contributed to an understanding of how the lives of tribal members have changed over the past 150 years.

During the summer, when I am running an excavation, I am sort of a jack-of-all-trades. I keep track of the actions of 5 to 25 excavators, take notes on the excavation's progress, record where all of the artifacts were found, check that supplies are sufficient, or give visitors a tour of the site. After an excavation is done for the day, I spend time sorting out the status of digs and planning how to proceed over the next few days.

Once an excavation is over, all of the artifacts are brought back to the lab. As a university professor, a majority of my time during the school

Mark Warner says he became hooked on archaeology in a 10-week field school.

year is spent teaching classes. I also spend a lot of time in the lab working with students who are continuing to analyze the artifacts that we excavated during the summer. I may help students catalog artifacts or offer suggestions on what to look for when identifying objects. For instance, I suggest where a particular ceramic fragment may have been manufactured, point out landmarks on a bone that aid in species identification, or indicate where cut marks modified a bone. After everything is analyzed, the excavation results are written up to tell the story we uncovered.

ANY ADVICE FOR STUDENTS?

The best way to learn about archaeology is to participate in an excavation. Almost without fail, students will discover whether archaeology is a passion by working on a dig and spending time getting their hands dirty—and most likely blistered! Students should also read about the field. Good starting points might be Charles Orser's textbook

Historical Archaeology or James Deetz's book *In Small Things Forgotten*. Or they can simply talk to a historical archaeologist.

A field archaeologist generally needs a bachelor's degree, so students should strongly consider going on to college. To be the person in charge, the principal investigator, the minimum education requirement is a master's degree. A doctorate is necessary to teach at a college or university.

WHY DO YOU LIKE THIS JOB?

The summer I became hooked on archaeology was the best of my life. Right after college I participated in a 10-week field school in northeastern New Mexico where I began to learn about archaeology. Since that first summer, every field project that I have been involved with has generated memorable experiences and recovered exciting artifacts. The key thing to keep in mind with archaeology is that finding bones, bottles, buttons, and ceramics are just a means to an end. The objects we find are interesting because of the story that they can tell about how people lived their lives.

I take great joy in two things: showing students another way of learning about the past aside from what is written in texts and contributing in a modest way to our understanding of the histories of people who tend to be overlooked in our books.

BONUS POINTS	EDUCATION	ON THE WEB	RELATED CAREERS
	BA, anthropology and government; MAA, master's of applied anthropology; PhD, anthropology	Society for Historical Archaeology (*www.sha.org*)	prehistoric archaeologist, forensic anthropologist, archivist, historian, historical research assistant, cultural artifact specialist, museum curator/technician, ethnologist

Let's Investigate

DINOSAUR PALEONTOLOGIST

In the hunt for dinosaurs, only a small number of species have been unearthed. Many answers remain buried, awaiting discovery, which is why dinosaur paleontology is such a thriving field today. Dinosaur paleontologist Matthew Carrano not only works with real dinosaur bones every day, but also contributes to the centuries-old process of furthering scientific understanding. To Carrano, it is always exciting to uncover a new dinosaur fossil and be the first person in the history of the universe to see and touch it.

DESCRIBE THIS JOB.

A paleontologist is any scientist who studies the remains of ancient life, as revealed in *fossils*—remains or traces of organisms that lived in the geological past and are preserved in Earth's crust. Dinosaur paleontologists specialize in the study of dinosaurs, as opposed to other kinds of extinct animals, and work as museum curators, college and university professors, or in other research- and education-focused jobs.

As the Curator of Dinosaurs at the Smithsonian Institution's National Museum of Natural History *(www.nmnh.si.edu/paleo/dinosaurs/index.htm)*, my work involves a lot of different tasks on a day-to-day basis. I conduct my own research program focused on the evolution of dinosaurs, which involves use of the museum collection and library, visits to other museums, fieldwork to collect new dinosaur fossils,

and publication of scientific papers. I also develop new exhibits, maintain existing ones, and lecture to the public and local universities. Finally, I care for the museum's collection of fossil reptiles and amphibians.

RECENT PROJECTS?

Two useful projects I have worked on are community service based. First, I created The Polyglot Paleontologist *(http://ravenel.si.edu/paleo/palegot/index.cfm)*, which collects hundreds of translated foreign-language paleontology papers and makes them available free for anyone to download. Second, I am compiling every dinosaur discovery ever published into the Paleobiology Database *(http://paleodb.org)*. When finished, it will allow anyone to access every piece of published information on dinosaur discoveries instantly.

Matthew Carrano inspects a fossil.

ADVICE FOR STUDENTS?

Generally, paleontologists are trained in geology and biology and have a master's or doctoral degree. Dinosaur paleontologists typically focus on biology, but I would strongly advise interested students to get a thorough training in both geology and biology—these two sciences are the foundation for all of paleontology. Other skills needed include math, statistics, geography, and computer proficiency. Depending on interest, additional training might involve illustration, physics, or chemistry.

Students can contact local museum, college, or university paleontologists to learn about volunteer opportunities and places to collect fossils. Students should take advantage of any opportunity to get field experience, such as geology camps, biology field trips, or local science clubs.

HOW DID YOU CHOOSE THIS FIELD?

When I think about how I got to where I am, I recall many small but significant milestones. Originally, I became interested in dinosaurs in second grade when I read the National Geographic book *Dinosaurs*. In high school, a biology teacher arranged for me to conduct research with an entomologist at Yale University's Peabody Museum of Natural History, but she gave me the wrong contact information. I instead called a paleontology graduate student who immediately offered me a project and, that summer, invited me into the field for a couple of weeks, where I found my first dinosaur bones.

In college, my biology professor helped transform my dinosaur "fan appreciation" into actual scientific interest. He taught me about scientific inquiry and encouraged me to present at a professional meeting, write a scientific paper, and apply for scholarships and grants. At the time, I didn't think any of those events seemed important, but now I realize that each incident proved crucial in my career path.

BONUS POINTS	EDUCATION	ON THE WEB	RELATED CAREERS
	BS, Geology-Biology; MS, PhD, Organismal Biology and Anatomy	Carrano's website *(www. nmnh.si.edu/paleo/curator_ cvs/carrano.html)*; Dinosauria Online *(www.dinosauria.com)*	geologist, biologist, museum educator, scientific illustrator

Let's Investigate

BONE DETECTIVE

We have all heard the expression "eyes are windows to our souls." Similarly, a forensic anthropologist might say "bones are windows to our lives." When someone dies and their identity is unknown, skeletal clues can uncover who that person is and the circumstances surrounding his or her death. Using scientific techniques, these bone detectives help solve cases involving unidentified victims from crimes, fires, plane crashes, wars, and accidents. Forensic anthropologist Diane France views her work as a series of puzzles as she helps law enforcement, medical examiners, and families piece together hard cases.

DESCRIBE THIS FIELD.

Forensic science, in general, is literally the application of science to answer legal questions. Forensic anthropology is a subfield of biological anthropology—the study of physical [biological] aspects of humans and nonhuman primates. So, forensic anthropology applies the scientific study of humans to answer legal questions.

In essence, if a deceased person is unidentifiable through methods such as dental comparisons and fingerprint analysis, a forensic anthropologist (FA) tries to figure out who that person is and the circumstances surrounding the death. We use various techniques to gather information. Primarily, we rely on skeletal clues, even if the body is relatively intact with soft tissue remaining. For instance, clues such as gunshot wounds, blunt trauma, and sharp injuries [such as knife wounds] are found by studying the skeleton directly and by viewing x-rays taken

postmortem [after death]. A person's photograph, taken antemortem [before death], can be compared to a skull in question—this method is used more to exclude individuals for further comparison than for positive identification. Some anthropologists apply a clay face to a skull using standard soft-tissue depth measurements. The media then puts that model in the newspapers and on television to see if anyone recognizes the face, which leads to hints about who the person might be.

HOW DID YOU CHOOSE THIS FIELD?

I have always loved science and been intrigued by bones; however, I began college thinking I wanted to be a marine biologist. I was taking required science courses in biology, chemistry, and physics, but I decided to branch off into general and biological anthropology for my elective courses.

Through my electives, I became hooked on human bones, which is how I ended up in forensic anthropology. It was not always easy—in graduate school I sometimes had to work three jobs while taking a full load of courses.

A TYPICAL DAY?

A typical day for an FA depends on the work environment [such as a university, federal government identification lab, or state crime lab]. I have an uncommon situation professionally. I started a small business 20 years ago that manufactures museum-quality plastic replicas of biological [primarily skeletal] materials for museums and universities, so I spend a significant amount of time working at that business every week. In addition, I am a private FA consultant; therefore, the forensic anthropology part of my day depends on the caseload. My caseload can range from no cases to mass fatality incidents such as plane crashes. I also write professional books and belong to a volunteer group that helps law enforcement look for clandestine graves and recover the evidence [including bodies] from those graves. I spend some time each week with that group—NecroSearch International, which consists of about 35 individuals with different fields of expertise—as we go all over the world helping law enforcement.

BACKGROUND NEEDED?

Classes in biological anthropology [including osteology], physics, chemistry, and human anatomy are essential. Also, classes that offer human soft-tissue dissections from donated bodies are recommended, although difficult to come by. Occasionally, a knowledge of culture is helpful in identification—for example, some cultures do things to their skeletons while alive that still show up after death—but for the most part, this field is biological in nature. An understanding of scientific inquiry is vitally important.

Obtaining a doctorate degree and becoming certified as an expert by the American Board of Forensic Anthropology (ABFA) are very helpful achievements; however, not everyone who practices forensic anthropology has taken these steps. To become certified, one has to have had a doctorate in biological anthropology or a closely related field for three years, have practiced enough in the field to submit five case reports to the ABFA for review, and then be invited to sit for eight-hour board exams. Although a pretty rigorous process, it is important for understanding the depth of knowledge necessary to be termed an expert. I am trained as an FA, have a doctorate in biological anthropology, and am certified as an expert in forensics.

ADVICE FOR STUDENTS?

There are two ways to tackle problems in human identification and determination of circumstances surrounding an individual's death. One approach is to memorize the numerous ways a body can react to physical stress and different biological environments. The other tactic—which is more interesting and fun, and makes a whole lot more sense—is to have the ample background needed to discover clues and determine how a body reacted to specific situations. The more courses students take in biology, physics, and, to some extent, chemistry, the more they will understand how the human body reacts to different situations [for example, how a bone would break given certain physical pressures in distinct areas].

Most important, students should be curious and observant about the world and everything in it. Students should also know early in the game if they can stand the sight of a decomposing body and if they are willing to get dirty while looking for clues. Real life forensic investigators, including law enforcement and scientific teams, do not work the jobs of television CSIs; we do not solve crimes in an hour and stay clean while simply shining flashlights on evidence.

MOST MEMORABLE EXPERIENCE?

Many experiences come to mind. I helped with the recovery process at the Fresh Kills Landfill on Staten Island after September 11, 2001. I have assisted with body identifications after plane crashes and after a forest fire in Colorado killed 12 young smoke jumpers. I have worked to find bodies of people [usually young women] who have been missing for decades and determined what happened to them. I went to Russia with NecroSearch and became involved in a controversy about whether or not the Russians have actually identified Anastasia [one of Czar Nicholas II daughters, incorrectly portrayed in the Disney film]. The Russians are still looking for the bodies of two of the Romanov children. By the way, the Russians state publicly and seem to believe that they have identified and buried Anastasia, but I believe they are probably still looking for Anastasia and Alexis [the son].

BONUS POINTS	EDUCATION	ON THE WEB	RELATED CAREERS
	BA, anthropology; MA, anthropology; PhD, biological anthropology; ABFA certification	American Board of Forensic Anthropology (www.csuchico.edu/anth/ABFA); NecroSearch International (www.necrosearch.org)	homicide investigator, fingerprint examiner, forensics (f.) technician, f. dentist, f. pathologist, f. psychologist, f. engineer, f. toxicologist, f. artist, f. entomologist

RESEARCH AND DEVELOPMENT

Research and Development

INDUSTRIAL TOXICOLOGIST

Are you ever curious about the safety of sugar substitutes, air pollution, or your city's tap water? Chemicals may make the world work, but some can be harmful—toxicologists can help us know which ones. They work in commercial industries, government health organizations, and research institutions to uncover, resolve, and communicate the hazardous effects chemicals may have on us and on our environment. As an industrial toxicologist with consumer products company Procter & Gamble (P&G), Greg Allgood has been responsible for ensuring the safety of products used by millions of people.

WHAT INSPIRED YOU TO BECOME A TOXICOLOGIST?

I became a toxicologist for two reasons: I wanted the challenge that comes with a multidisciplinary career, and I wanted to contribute to public health. The field of toxicology requires me to be knowledgeable in many different areas including nutrition, biochemistry, microbiology, pathology, mechanistic toxicology, and physiology. I have found that the best breakthroughs in research come from combining unexpected areas of expertise. To paraphrase Einstein, you cannot solve a problem with the same thinking that created it. When earning my master's degree in public health, I realized my passion to do work that helped society. That passion led me to pursue a doctorate in toxicology. I now work on projects that use my

company's technologies to significantly improve the quality of life in developing countries.

DESCRIBE YOUR WORK.

Because of my broad background in toxicology, I initially became a member of the team responsible for ensuring the safety of P&G's nutritional products [a food toxicologist]. For example, I would evaluate food additives to determine if any ingredients had the potential to cause cancer, birth defects, or neurological toxicity. During that time I actually appeared on the *Oprah Winfrey Show* to talk about a well-known fat replacement, Olestra, which was pretty exciting! Over time, I found that I could contribute more in a broad range of roles, including that of a clinical scientist, regulatory expert, and head of our medical surveillance group. Now I am

94

the associate director of P&G's safe drinking water project. The project's water-purifying technologies help to address a chief source of sickness and death in our world's children—unsafe water.

PLEASE DESCRIBE A TYPICAL WORKDAY.

That is what I love about my job: There is no "typical" day. During the past few months, I have traveled to destinations worldwide in search of ways to implement our safe drinking water technology. I have presented our research at the United Nations Headquarters in New York, spoken with the vice president of Pakistan, and talked with consumers living in dirt huts in Haiti and remote parts of Kenya. With global relief groups, I've worked to help the humanitarian crisis caused by the floods in Bangladesh, Haiti, and the Dominican Republic as well as aided Sudanese refugees in Chad who suffer from devastating malnutrition attributed in part to diarrhea caused by unsafe drinking water. Visiting the homes of people benefiting from our safe drinking water project and seeing the children who are better off now than they were before is very rewarding.

Greg Allgood's work on safe drinking water takes him all over the world.

ANY ADVICE FOR STUDENTS?

Students should explore university websites to learn about various toxicology programs. To find out more about safe drinking water work and other leading health-care technologies that focus on improving quality of life, students can visit P&G Health Sciences Institute's website at *www.pghsi.com*. Participation in advanced science classes, such as biology and chemistry, allows students to measure their love of science. A student's present degree of patience and aptitude with research projects can be an indication of how well he or she will respond to the failures and rewards of industry research.

BONUS POINTS	EDUCATION	ON THE WEB	RELATED CAREERS
	BS, biology; MSPH (master's of science in public health); PhD, toxicology	Society of Toxicology (*www.toxicology.org*); World Health Organization (*www.who.int/en*); Centers for Disease Control and Prevention (*www.cdc.gov*)	microbiologist, nutritionist, epidemiologist, pathologist, biomedical laboratory technician

Research and Development

COATINGS SPECIALIST

Your omelet did not stick to your pan this morning, and water beaded on your car as you drove out of the car wash. What makes this happen? Coatings. The majority of everyday objects, from jacket buttons to cars, have some sort of coating. The coating on the faucet in your kitchen, for instance, makes the faucet resistant to corrosion from the chemicals and abrasives found in cleaners used around the sink. These coatings are designed by scientists such as Patrick Sullivan, senior scientist in the Research and Development Department at Vapor Technologies. Sullivan applies a process called physical vapor deposition (PVD) to build coatings. The relationship between energy and matter is central to this process. Sullivan uses energy to convert solid metal into a gas, which then condenses as a solid coating (a thin film) on objects that we use every day.

WHAT INSPIRED YOU TO BECOME INVOLVED IN PVD AND COATINGS?

In some ways, my path naturally evolved. In high school, math came easily, so it followed that a career in engineering would be appropriate. However, the university I attended on a basketball scholarship did not offer an engineering program, so I majored in physics. I continued and earned a PhD in engineering physics and materials science but ultimately became more interested in practical physics than in basic research. I left academia to join a company that helps create real products such as sunglasses, skis, and doorknobs. I like creating consumer products—things that people actually use.

HOW DO YOU USE MATTER AND ENERGY IN YOUR CAREER?

My company employs Vacuum Arc, a particular PVD process. In this procedure, a large chamber is loaded with parts to be coated. The chamber is then closed, and air is pumped out, creating a vacuum. Then, an inert gas, argon, is fed into the chamber. Subsequently, a high current is applied to create an arc across a gap between the chamber walls and a solid metal rod. The intense, dense energy from the arc evaporates the metal rod, changing the metal from a solid state to liquid to gas. Charged atoms ejected from the metal rod collide with the argon atoms, creating plasma—

matter in an energetic, gas state. The plasma creates a conductive path that sustains the arc in the vacuum. As the evaporation occurs, parts—such as faucets—are rotated in front of this evaporating source. The gas condenses on the parts growing a thin solid film atom by atom.

HOW ARE COATINGS USED?

Coatings are responsible for limiting heat transfer through windows of skyscrapers; reflecting UV [ultraviolet] light from lenses on sunglasses; optimizing optics on cameras and flat screen displays; and reflecting images from mirrors. Other examples of coatings are thin films applied to protect integrated circuits used in cellular phones, computers, DVD players, cars, and airplanes.

My company applies decorative and durable coatings and sells coating equipment. Our coatings are on faucets, drill bits, dental tools, and bike shocks, for example. Often these coatings are sold with a lifetime guarantee; so, in addition to having an appealing and uniform look, they must be durable. Coatings can help delay corrosion and decay of a product.

Sullivan likes creating consumer products—things that people actually use.

DESCRIBE A TYPICAL DAY.

It usually includes meetings with customers or employees, writing a report, some analysis of data, and perhaps some experiments. I am a project manager, which means I guide the research and people on specific projects. About half the days, an urgent, unforeseen issue will arise and change the daily plan. For example, sometimes I have to determine the cause of discoloration occurring on a batch of doorknobs from our PVD process. We use several tools that measure composition, structure, and texture to analyze samples. Essentially, I enjoy solving challenging problems and working with nifty analytical tools.

BONUS POINTS	EDUCATION	ON THE WEB	RELATED CAREERS
	BS, physics; PhD, engineering physics and materials science	American Physical Society *(www.aps.org)*; Bose-Einstein Condensation *(www.colorado.edu/ physics/PhysicsInitiative/ Physics2000.05.98/bec)*	chemist, chemical engineer, electrical engineer, materials scientist

Research and Development

MICROBIOLOGIST

Although invisible to the naked eye, viruses, bacteria, fungi, and parasites can be found everywhere, from the air we breathe to inside our favorite foods. Microbiologists investigate how these organisms exist and affect our lives. Dale B. Emeagwali is renowned for her contributions to the field of microbiology; in fact, in 1996 she received the Scientist of the Year Award from the National Technical Association, which recognizes researchers whose discoveries have benefited humankind. Among those discoveries, Emeagwali, a faculty member of Morgan State University, demonstrated that the expression of Ras oncogene—the most common culprit in human cancers—could be inhibited by antisense methodology—the use of small molecules to prevent the oncoprotein from being made and thereby suppressing tumor formation. Emeagwali attributes her best experiences to working on a variety of organisms and problems, which has allowed her to always bring a fresh perspective to her work.

WHAT INSPIRED YOU TO BECOME A MICROBIOLOGIST?

My parents introduced me to scientific concepts early on through simple questions and experiments. I decided to major in biology in college, which is when I had my first microbiology course. The study of microorganisms was fascinating. I was particularly captivated by the large variety of bacteria. Also, experiments and results are attained quickly with bacteria because they grow at such a rapid rate. They can multiply every 20 to 40 minutes. Often results can be produced the same or next day. In graduate school, I focused on bacteria that grow in soil. Subsequently, I studied other microbes as well, such as viruses and protozoans.

DESCRIBE YOUR WORK.

Microbiologists study microscopic organisms, of which there are many. Because the field is so broad, microbiologists tend to specialize in areas or organisms—for example, virology, bacteriology, parasitology, mycology [study of fungi], and immunology [study of the body's defense against disease]. And microbiologists work just about everywhere. They can be found working as researchers, technicians, teachers, and administrators in hospitals, research institutions, government laboratories, educational institutions, and in the biotechnology industry. Some experienced microbiologists may also choose to use their expertise in safety programs, policy making, or legal

98

fields. The overall goal of my work has always been to answer fundamental questions about cellular processes. I also like my work to have potentially significant applications in the medical field. Thus, my interests lead me to conduct research in various areas including microbial physiology, virology, biochemistry, and molecular biology. A typical day involves checking on previous experiments, setting up new investigations, and analyzing data. While I find my work fun, it does get busy at times. The reward of obtaining new data makes it worth the effort. In addition to laboratory research, time must also be spent writing papers and reading to keep up with new developments.

Dale Emeagwali became interested in microorganisms in college.

WHAT EDUCATIONAL BACKGROUND AND SKILLS ARE NEEDED?

All science and math courses offered in high school are required to prepare for a bachelor's degree in microbiology or biology. A bachelor's degree can lead to various research positions. Communication skills are also important, because microbiologists must be able to clearly write research results and give oral presentations. A master's degree increases career options in laboratory management, marketing, sales, and teaching. A doctoral degree is usually required for higher-level positions in government laboratories, universities, and industry. Also, keeping abreast of new breakthroughs is important because the field is constantly changing. I also believe that everyone, especially scientists, should be well read in a broad spectrum of subjects. An interdisciplinary approach to problem solving improves critical thinking, and scientific discoveries increase as different fields merge. To learn more about microbiology, students should visit a library and the American Society for Microbiology *(www. asm.org)* website. A passion for the subject, a burning desire to answer a question, and an interest in the outcome are essential.

	EDUCATION	ON THE WEB	RELATED CAREERS
BONUS POINTS	BS, biology; minor in chemistry; PhD, microbiology	The American Society for Microbiology (*www.asm. org*)	laboratory technician, biology teacher, clinical trials manager, physician assistant, biotechnologist, environmental scientist, mycologist

Research and Development

PERFUMER

The bonds between chemistry and perfumery are considerable. To understand the whys and hows of perfumery—the interactions that occur within the nose and among the molecules within a fragrance itself—one must understand the essence of substances and how they behave in different conditions. But perfumery is not just a science. It is an art, and it allows Christophe Laudamiel [a fine fragrance-toiletries perfumer with International Flavors and Fragrances, Inc.] to engage his passion for chemistry and fragrances creatively. Laudamiel bottles inspiration and makes it tangible. Even people who interact every day with perfumers know little about how this transformation transpires.

WHAT INSPIRED YOU TO BECOME A PERFUMER?

My nose was unconsciously trained from a young age. Cooking in my family was always a ritual. We spent hours searching wild forests and mountains for berries, fruit, mushrooms, and edible flowers to make family recipes. Our garden itself bore an extensive collection of tulips and roses. I recall reading magazines and books on the 100 different varieties of heirloom apples in ancient France, the benefit of orange bigarade buds [terrible taste, great scent], and which tulip to plant where. Raised in France with this foundation of ingredients and fragrances, throughout my childhood I wanted to become a chef.

At age 14, I started chemistry classes in school. I became passionate for the subject—it encompasses everything one touches on this Earth. The study of matter and the changes it undergoes reminded me of cooking. But chemistry was no day in the kitchen; it was very rational and powerful. I went on to receive a master's degree in chemistry and then began an internship at Procter & Gamble in flavor chemistry [developing flavors with natural and artificial ingredients]. Everything crystallized. After a few months at the company, I was drawn to perfumery because of the greater variety of fragrance aromas. I received my perfumer-creator degree from Procter & Gamble in 1997 and became a senior perfumer there.

WHAT DOES A PERFUMER DO?

Perfumers tend to specialize in one of two categories: fine fragrance-toiletries or functional. Fine fragrance perfumers create perfumes for fashion houses. Functional perfumers design scents for products such as shampoos, detergents, and antiperspirants. Most fashion houses today do not have perfumers in-house. Rather, different fragrance houses compete for the opportunity to create a product, much like interior designers make a design bid for a project.

A perfumer has several clients to compete for simultaneously. Each project involves creating a fragrance formula, be it for a perfume found in department stores or a detergent used to wash clothes. A formula contains 40 to 100 ingredients of both natural and new [manufactured] molecules. Designing a fragrance and combining the molecules is comparable to composing sheet music—writing it, playing it [for example, smelling it on various mediums and testing the diffusion of materials], starting afresh, reviewing it, and challenging it until both the creative team and client are pleased and the fragrance does the job. Some creations are very commercial, some more original. The inspirations differ as much as the clients' desires and dreams differ.

Participating in and leading strategy meetings with a laboratory [an entire lab is needed to support a perfume's creation] or clients is also part of the job. I must always keep my creativity and inspiration alive. Therefore, I study and research natural ingredients and new molecules to compare and evaluate them hedonistically [to determine how pleasurable or interesting a scent is] and for performance. Perfumers must also be well informed of fluctuations in supply or cost of materials. For instance, an Indonesian crisis created a drop in supply of patchouli oil, and the little oil available became outrageously expensive. There

Christophe Laudamiel uses his strong background in chemistry in his job as a perfumer.

are no manufactured molecules currently available to replace patchouli oil, which contains in itself around 200 molecules.

HOW DO YOU USE SCIENCE?

A strong background in chemistry works miracles. The mystery and myriad of scents found in perfumes actually have very rational explanations based on concepts such as volatilities, Van der Waals interactions, hydrogen bonds, and chemical reactions between alcohols, aldehydes, and amines. My science knowledge is also useful when observing diffusion theories on paper, skin, and fabrics. A chemist-perfumer can more thoroughly participate in research programs with chemists to discover new molecules that result in innovative scents for the 21st century. I am actually one of the rare perfumers to have patents on manufactured molecules and new diffusion techniques.

The biggest challenge of perfumery is the lack of prediction. The explanations are always found after the facts. Traditionally, scents are classified as notes based on their olfactory character. Top notes are detected and fade first, providing freshness [such as light scents that are usually citrus or wet greens lasting 5–30 minutes]. Middle notes last sometimes a few hours and are the most prominent within the fragrance [usually combinations of floral, spicy, or fruit scents]. Base notes give a perfume depth, last the longest, and are generally musky or woodsy notes. This classification of top, middle, and base notes designed to give a particular harmony is presently being challenged with a more exact approach.

In music, a "ti" note will always sound like a "ti," independently of the note played before and the one played after. This is close to impossible in perfumery. Even after 30 years of successful creations, experienced perfumers are down to trial and error when combining notes. This is explained by basic chemistry principles such as the second principle of thermodynamics. To predict the influence of a material in a mixture containing 60 other ingredients is difficult because of the real versus ideal chemical potentials in thermodynamics. The possibilities are endless, 1,000 to 2,000 scents are available to use in a fragrance, and they may be dosed at different magnitudes within the fragrance depending on the desired effect. Also, a molecule from one supplier smells different from the same molecule from another supplier due to the smallest amount of impurities derived from different synthesis routes or starting materials. In terms of natural molecules, a bergamot from southeastern Italy smells different from a bergamot from southwestern Italy. The nose, even a layperson's, is very sensitive.

The complexity and molecular design of chemistry triggering a scent perception in the nose is as elaborate as the chemistry necessary for a drug to trigger a response on a specific organ. Specifically, whether an isomer is cis, trans, or chiral is crucial because one structural difference of a molecular formula can completely change the olfactive or diffusive character. It could mean the difference between a vanilla scent and the odor in a dentist's office.

ANY ADVICE FOR STUDENTS?

Today, a background in chemistry is often required to enter a perfume university program or a perfumery school within a fragrance company. The bottom line is to work hard to learn all the materials, train your nose, and learn how to create. Then, as in any art, a certain sensibility, curiosity, humility, passion, and some would say a little gift, are absolutely necessary to make a difference. Just like the ear, the nose gets trained with practice.

BONUS POINTS	EDUCATION MS, chemistry; Perfumer-Creator Degree	ON THE WEB The International Fragrance Association (www.ifraorg.org); Sense of Smell Institute (www.senseofsmell.org)	RELATED CAREERS food scientist, lab technician, chemistry professor, color development chemist, chef, flavor chemist

Research and Development

GREEN PRODUCT CHEMIST

Green chemistry is the design of chemical products and processes that reduce, recycle, or eliminate the use and generation of hazardous substances. The fundamental idea of green chemistry is that the designer of a chemical is responsible for considering what will happen to the world after the product is introduced. Nike product chemist Andy Chen uses green chemistry to develop materials for apparel, equipment, and footwear that are healthy for workers, consumers, and the environment.

DESCRIBE YOUR WORK.

The Environmental Protection Agency's (EPA) Green Chemistry Program (GCP) is the driving force behind pollution prevention through the environmentally conscious design of chemical products and processes. Consistent with GCP's emphasis on fostering the use of healthier materials and processes, I help research, develop, and implement products that are better for the environment and human health, as well as scientifically sound and cost-effective.

All of our green products avoid using problematic chemicals—for example, Azo dyes, chromium VI, dioxins, disperse dyes, formaldehyde, lead, and pesticides—found on our company's Restricted Substances List (RSL).

As we research how to use green chemicals and remove problematic chemicals with respect to our products, we find new solutions for environmental, safety, and health (ESH) issues in our factories. For instance, we eliminate the need for expensive processes related to chemical disposal, emissions, and cleanup. Furthermore, the exploration of green chemistry opens up a new source of inspiration for product design. So, in the end, we develop environmentally preferred materials (EMP) that not only reduce ESH issues, but result in innovative, cost-effective, and healthier products for consumers.

A GREENER RUBBER.

As a product chemist, one of my most rewarding accomplishments was participating in the development of Nike's green rubber. To create this greener alternative, our goal was, whenever possible, to replace traditionally used problematic substances with naturally sourced materials. To start, we identified "red-alert chemicals," including health and environmental hazards, skin sensitizers, and potential allergens. We then experimented to find new formulations that would avoid the hazards but still maintain top-level performance and comparable cost. In the end, we removed four out of five problematic chemicals and reduced toxic chemicals by 96% in terms of weight.

Creating this EPM proved to be an exciting challenge and a major success. It was a big leap forward for the shoe industry and can be for other industries, such as tire manufacturers. To further promote a sustainable environment, I shared the green-rubber experience at the U.S. EPA Green Chemistry Conference.

ADVICE FOR STUDENTS?

Basic science training including math, biology, physics, and chemistry is important [my background is in chemistry, specifically]. Beyond that, good communication skills are critical for sharing ideas. Also, product chemists need to be willing to roll up their sleeves and really get involved in the work. With green chemistry, in particular, finding solutions to potential challenges requires creativity, enthusiasm for trying new things, and forward-thinking vision. Students should look around them and notice how much function, color, weight, performance, and even features connected to the digital world play in the design of shoes today. Students can think about how different contemporary shoes are from the ones their parents wore as kids, and imagine the changes still to come.

JOB SATISFACTION?

We are all aware of global warming and other environmental issues facing our planet. As a society, we need to clean up, rethink, and redesign both the materials we use and the way we manufacture. Personally, I would like to do as much as possible to provide our consumers with healthier products and leave the next generation a more sustainable world. I am proud to be part of pioneering work in this area.

BONUS POINTS	EDUCATION BS, chemistry; PhD, chemistry	ON THE WEB EPA's Green Chemistry Program *(www.epa.gov/ greenchemistry)*; American Apparel and Footwear Association RSL *(www. apparelandfootwear. org/Resources/ RestrictedSubstances.asp)*	RELATED CAREERS lab technician, chemical engineer, environmental engineer, product creation engineer, consumer products engineer

104

Research and Development

COSMETIC CHEMIST

Where do you turn when you have a bad hair day or need to cover up an unwanted blemish? From hair gels to concealers, cosmetic chemists use science and creativity to develop products that make us look and feel good. As the executive director of Chanel's Research and Development Formulation Laboratories, cosmetic chemist Amy Wyatt finds it exciting and rewarding to create useful, safe, and appealing personal care and pampering products.

DESCRIBE THIS FIELD.

In some ways, the process of formulating a cosmetic product is similar to cooking. With a scientific mind and an artistic eye, a cosmetic chemist carefully selects approved ingredients for an experimental formula. The ingredients can vary from natural or organic to highly advanced manmade substances. Ingredients must be evaluated and tweaked until the exact, desired product is achieved. This formulating expertise is gained over time through lab experience.

Chemists in this field can specialize in various areas. For instance, skin-care chemists create products such as cleansers and moisturizing lotions. With an eye for color, makeup chemists formulate decorative cosmetics such as lipsticks, foundations, and eye liners. Toiletry or fragrance-ancillary chemists focus on products such as body washes and lotions that support companies' signature fragrances. Hair-care chemists develop shampoos, conditioners, and fixative products such as gels.

SATISFACTION AT WORK?

Before I entered the cosmetics industry, I never considered where all of my skincare, makeup, and hair products came from. My first job out of college involved working as a technician in a printing and publishing lab. Fortunately, this lab experience, along with my bachelor's degree in biology, helped me land a cosmetic chemist position with Aveda. I immediately fell in love with the fast-paced field. I recall the challenge and excitement of creating my first product—an SPF 15 lip balm made with naturally derived ingredients. It was extremely gratifying to witness people actually buying something I made.

Working for Chanel, I am always thrilled to see the products I helped develop advertised in magazines and on television, as well as used by celebrities and other customers. Aside from product development, my career has led to many interesting experiences. For instance, because my company is international, I have traveled to Europe, Japan, and throughout most of the United States. I also appeared on a *MTV House of Style* video to demonstrate how to make lipstick and powder products.

THE GOAL OF CREATING SAFE, APPEALING PRODUCTS.

It is my responsibility to ensure that our research and development team creates high quality, exciting, and luxurious products on time and in budget. This includes guiding the development of projects, managing personnel, establishing project budgets, and coaching and mentoring my team. I must also make certain the final products pass strict stability and safety testing; like many other cosmetic companies, we use alternative in-vitro safety testing rather than animal testing. As an international company, our products must be globally compliant with regulatory requirements,

free of patent infringement, and proven to meet claims we are making. I work closely with other groups in the company [for example colleagues in quality assurance and marketing] and with my global counterparts in France and Japan.

ANY ADVICE FOR STUDENTS?

Most scientists working in this field have undergraduate and graduate degrees in chemistry, or a related science discipline. Chemistry is important to understand how ingredients will work together. Biology is needed to understand the effect of products on skin or hair. Physics, math, and engineering knowledge come in handy when scaling up the product through each stage of development: from the laboratory sample to the pilot quantity and then finally to the full-manufacturing volume.

To learn more about working in cosmetic chemistry, students can arrange informational interviews with scientists working in the industry and seek internships with cosmetics companies. Contacting the Society of Cosmetic Chemists is a good place to start.

BONUS POINTS	EDUCATION	ON THE WEB	RELATED CAREERS
	BS, biology	Society of Cosmetic Chemists *(www.scconline.org)*	perfumer, food technologist, microbiologist, quality-control chemist, technical salesperson, textile chemist

TECHNOLOGY— AND TOYS

VIDEO GAME LEVEL DESIGNER

For video gamers, here's something to chew on—those hours spent finely tuning your favorite pastime skills could lead to a cool career. From sound engineers to programmers, a whole slew of opportunities awaits you in video game development. Gaming was always a hobby for John Feil, until he landed a dream job in game level design at LucasArts—the company that makes Star Wars games. While Feil combines his interests, artistic talent, and technical skills to make something that entertains people, his job is not all fun and games. A designer's challenge is to create games with realistic environments; making things appear real requires knowledge of subjects ranging from geology and physics to biology and sociology. The places and levels you visit in a game would seem fake without influence from bona fide science.

DESCRIBE THIS JOB.

A video game level designer creates the individual missions found in a game. The responsibilities vary from game to game, but in most cases we create and place things that players may encounter, such as buildings, people, plants, and animals. We also have to program how the entities in different levels react to the player. Will the puppy run over and greet the player with a big slurp, or will he run away when the player comes near? By placing objects and instructing them how to act, the level designer creates an environment players can easily imagine as real.

HOW DO YOU USE SCIENCE?

Creating a realistic world requires knowledge about subjects such as geology, biology, sociology, anthropology, astronomy, geography, mathematics, and physics. For instance, if the player falls off a building, he cannot fall lightly like a leaf; the player must fall like a person affected by gravity. Even with little physics knowledge, a player knows what it looks like when a person falls. Because the player also understands that falling will hurt, we use biology principles to simulate injury. Similarly, computer-controlled people must behave and react realistically, so we need to know something about psychology. How those people act when they are in a group requires some knowledge of sociology and anthropology. The terrain that the player walks on also needs to make sense, so we need to be familiar with geology and geography.

WHAT BACKGROUND IS NEEDED?

At this point, the game industry is still pretty new, so there is not just one way to get into the business. I was a music major in college, for instance. Designers I know have been trained as architects, mechanical engineers, theologians, biologists, artists, and computer programmers. But times are changing. Hundreds of schools in the United States are developing [or already offering] degrees in game-related majors. A lot of people want to make games, however, so there is much competition. To get

John Feil uses science to make his game worlds seem real.

ahead, students should be familiar with principles across many disciplines—once again, we make worlds, so to make good games it is important to read a lot, pay attention in science and humanities courses, and know how the world works. While playing games, students should consider and analyze what is realistic, as well as when they are having fun, when they are not, and why. Last, but certainly not least, students should love video games.

	EDUCATION	ON THE WEB	RELATED CAREERS
BONUS POINTS	BS, music	International Game Developers Association *(www.igda.org)*	game sound engineer, game composer, fiction writer, game tester, computer programmer, animator

Technology—and Toys

AUTOMOTIVE TECHNICIAN

A knack for tinkering, fixing widgets, and solving problems are only the nuts and bolts required to work with the integrated electronic systems and complex computers that run our automobiles. The automotive technicians of today are diagnostic, high-tech problem solvers who must understand how vehicles' components work and interact. Science—particularly physics and including math—are essential to this understanding. Arcadio Mora, an automotive technician with Fuller Ford in California, was fascinated with cars while growing up. As a kid, he would man the toolbox while his father overhauled engines and performed maintenance on their family vehicles. When he won the 2003 National Ultimate Master Challenge, Mora was considered the best Ford technician in the country. He owes this great accomplishment to a lot of dedication, training, good working habits, and the willingness to go that extra mile.

DESCRIBE A TYPICAL DAY.

I arrive to work around 7:30 a.m. and have a brief meeting with the service manager about the goals and agenda for the day. I look over repair orders and put them in a logical order by time promised and calculated completion time. Once I bring the vehicle into the garage, I attempt to verify the owner's concern. We always look at the history of the vehicle and run a report through Ford to identify any common concerns, special service messages, recalls, or technical service bulletins. Once we determine what is wrong with the car and what caused it, we perform and verify the repair, fill out the work order, and then proceed to the next

vehicle. Every job is different, so there is always a new challenge. I am the shop foreman and therefore help other technicians solve problems. The day can be short if you're busy and everything goes smoothly, but some days are very challenging and frustrating. Those are the days I learn more.

HOW DO YOU USE SCIENCE?

Science, especially physics, is necessary to understand force, friction, hydraulics, and electrical circuits. Electricity is used for a car's heat, light, and motion. The vehicle's climate control system exists for passenger comfort. The car's interior can absorb heat from the Sun, engine, exhaust, pavement, and the passengers themselves. These sources transfer heat by radiation, conduction, or convection. Heat and humidity are removed in the air conditioning system by changing the state of the refrigerant from liquid to vapor [achieved by creating low and high pressures with compressors, fixed orifices, and heat transfers].

Kinetic energy (KE) keeps a vehicle in motion, and the brake system changes the KE into heat energy using the friction created when the brake pads are pressed against the rotor. Changing the applied pressure can vary the friction between these parts.

Generators produce an AC [alternating current] voltage, which is rectified into a DC [direct current] voltage. Generators convert mechanical energy into electrical energy and operate on the principle of magnetic induction. We use a battery to store energy in a chemical form, provide electricity to power all systems, and help stabilize voltage once the vehicle is running.

Engines are designed to function at certain operating temperatures. We use coolant to raise the boiling point of water, which also lowers the freezing point of water. Pressurizing the cooling system also increases water's boiling point. For

Arcadio Mora, center, won Ford's 2003 National Ultimate Master Challenge.

every pound of pressure, we increase the boiling point -16°C. You have probably heard not to open the radiator cap when the engine is hot. Once you open the cap, you lose the pressure and, if the coolant is somewhere around 100°C or higher, it's going to boil and shoot out.

ANY ADVICE FOR HIGH SCHOOL STUDENTS?

Finish high school. There is not much you can do without a high school diploma. Science, math, and computer classes are needed to understand, analyze, and solve problems. If there is an automobile class in your high school, attend it. The automotive instructors usually have more than just book knowledge. Pick their brains.

BONUS POINTS	EDUCATION	ON THE WEB	RELATED CAREERS
	High school diploma	Automotive Student Service Educational Training (*www.fordasset.com*); Ford Accelerated Credential Training (*www.factuti.com*)	industrial truck mechanic, engineer, aircraft technician

Technology—and Toys

ROLLER COASTER DESIGNER

Thrill rides, scream machines, loop-de-loops, colossal peaks, and heart-stopping drops. Roller coasters may seem to defy all laws of physics, but do not let that sense of danger fool you. A coaster gains potential energy as it is pulled to the top of the highest hill, which changes to kinetic energy as the coaster begins its descent. Once the coaster is under way, gravity, velocity, friction, and acceleration are just a few of the physics principles controlling the ride. Although coasters are designed to be a frightening experience for passengers, in reality they are safer than crossing the street. Roller coaster designers like Kent Seko create these dynamic rides, which simulate such a genuine air of peril.

WHAT INSPIRED YOU TO BECOME A ROLLER COASTER DESIGNER?

I actually have a bachelor's degree in geography from the University of Utah. My true aspiration was to become an architect. Because architecture was not available as an undergraduate degree, I took pre-architecture classes as electives. Many of these classes focused on design, which has helped me in the amusement industry. After college, a downturn in the architecture job market caused me to look for employment opportunities in other fields. I responded to an advertisement for Arrow Dynamics, the largest designer and manufacturer of amusement rides at the time, and was given a chance as an entry-level drafter. The scale and speed of the roller coasters being designed were

mind-blowing. We were just completing the first 60.96 m tall roller coaster during my first year of employment—a major threshold for coasters at that time. There are now rides over 91.44 m tall. Several years into my employment at Arrow I was offered the opportunity to learn the ins and outs, or should I say the ups and downs, of coaster design. Fifteen years later I am still with the same company [now S & S-Arrow, LLC]. I have gained a lot of education through experience working in this field with some of the most knowledgeable people in the industry.

WHAT DOES A COASTER DESIGNER DO?

The goal is to design the most exciting ride while meeting all specifications defined by a client within a budget. Safety, of course, is of utmost impor-

tance. I spend a majority of my time designing and drawing models on a computer. More often than not, my company is competing with other ride manufacturers to land a project. As part of a design team, I work closely with the marketing department to make sure we are meeting a prospective client's requirements. After a design has been finalized, the engineering stage of the project takes place to build and assemble all components of the ride. There is a lot of coordination that must go on between engineers, designers, and drafters during this stage of the project.

Kent Seko got into roller coaster design with his background in architecture, but he says engineering is key.

WHAT ADVICE WOULD YOU GIVE TO AN INTERESTED HIGH SCHOOL STUDENT?

I often receive inquiries from individuals who want to get involved with the amusement industry. I always tell them to study hard in school, particularly in math and physics. Unfortunately, there is no university of roller coaster design. Anyone interested in employment with a ride manufacturer should major in engineering in college—structural engineering if a student is interested in ride layout design or the design of the structure to support a roller coaster, mechanical engineering if a student is interested in designing the vehicles or other mechanical components of a roller coaster. Additionally, electrical engineers are required to design the control system of a roller coaster.

BONUS POINTS	EDUCATION	ON THE WEB	RELATED CAREERS
	BS, geography	International Association of Amusement Parks and Attractions *(www.iaapa.org)*	architect, interior designer, graphic artist, electronic technician, aerospace engineer, drafter

ARTIFICIAL INTELLIGENCE EXPERT

From assembly lines to trash collection to space exploration, robots play an increasingly important role in our lives. We may think of robots as entertainment, a fun hobby, or tools used to perform repetitive, precise, and hazardous tasks, but researchers of artificial intelligence (AI)—the study of how computer systems can simulate intelligent processes—see robots in another light. AI researchers, such as Ruth Aylett, professor of intelligent virtual environments at the University of Salford in the United Kingdom, appreciate robots as a way to understand human intelligence and basic interaction. Aylett is the author of *Robots: Bringing Intelligent Machines to Life*.

WHAT ARE ROBOTS?

Robots can be used to copy or improve upon human performance, undertake tasks dangerous for humans, or even provide a way to understand human intelligence in its primary function—interaction. At the most basic level, robots are composed of several systems working together. Movements are directed by a brain, the controller. The body, tools, and mobility are unique to the robot's task [for example, a robot uses propellers and rudders in the water, and legs or wheels on land]. Power fuels the robot [electric solar cells are one example]. Sensors provide signals to give robots a perceptual understanding of their environment so they can alter their behaviors based on that information.

HOW ARE ROBOTS USED?

Can machines multitask and rely on humanlike senses successfully? To look at these questions, I studied cooperation with robots Fred and Ginger, which were developed to carry objects around together. The object they carried acted as a message between the two robots: If Ginger sped up or moved away from Fred, sensors located on Ginger would tell her that the object was off-center, and she would then slow down or switch directions accordingly. Likewise, Fred would speed up or move toward Ginger to re-center the object.

Robots can be autonomous, or capable of functioning independently. For example, autonomous robot cleaners are very effective and work like vacuum cleaners. There are small models for homes and waist-height models for large-scale buildings, such as stadiums. Their popularity is limited mainly because human labor is still more cost-efficient. Robots can also be used as surgical assistants. In drilling small holes in bone for hip replacement joints, for example, robots, unlike humans, will not shake and are more precise. Surgeons are concerned, nevertheless, about putting their responsibility for a human life in the "hands" of a robot assistant. Hospital robots [which carry objects through corridors] and robot museum guides have also encountered problems. Both are designed with obstacle avoidance sensors but have ended up cornered and made immobile by curious spectators.

ADVICE FOR STUDENTS?

Just as robots are made of several systems, the field of AI requires a collaboration of many different disciplines for success. Engineering is clearly useful. AI researchers have backgrounds in computer science, biology, psychology, physics, linguistics, physics, neuroscience, and even philosophy. Students should be willing to learn a lot of new things from a variety of disciplines. To learn more about AI and robotics, students should read *Creation: Life and How to Make It* by Steve Grand, and Stan Franklin's *Artificial Minds*. Students can form a small group and enter a competition, such as RoboCup. Building a robot is an excellent, interdisciplinary, team-building project. As students learn more about AI and robots, they will realize the improbability of sci-fi dramatizations about robots taking over the universe. For one thing, robot motors use a lot of power and usually last about 30 minutes to 2 hours before needing recharging.

HOW DID YOU BECOME INVOLVED IN AI?

In high school I took a lot of math and science courses. I realized that many scientific concepts were understood and demonstrated through the development of models—for example, our model of the solar system helps us understand many details involving Earth and other planets. I also spent a lot of time pondering key concepts in psychology, particularly human intelligence. I wondered if it was possible to make a model of intelligence to better understand actual human intelligence. Specifically, if we can build something that's intelligent, then our ideas about the concept are not just theories. So, when I discovered AI in the early 1980s, it was just what I'd been looking for.

BONUS POINTS	EDUCATION Engineering Council Chartered Engineer; degree in mathematical economics (British degrees)	ON THE WEB American Association for Artificial Intelligence (*www. aaai.org)*; RoboCup (*www. robocup.org/02.html*)	RELATED CAREERS aerospace engineer, inventor, computer programmer, video game designer, software developer

Technology—and Toys

SPACE ARCHITECT

Drawing knowledge from many fields—including science, engineering, and art—space architects such as Constance Adams design structures for nonterrestrial environments. In one such project at NASA, Adams works on elements for the International Space Station (ISS), which is currently being assembled, and inhabited, in outer space. For Adams, and everyone involved with ISS, each week brings new, unanticipated challenges as scientists learn about the orbital environment 330 km above Earth and what it takes to exist there.

DESCRIBE YOUR WORK.

An architect is trained as a generalist, whose job it is to understand not only the engineering and technical requirements of a project but the aesthetic and functional/operational aspects as well. With this knowledge, we analyze the requirements of a structure; create a design concept to meet technical, aesthetic, and functional needs; develop a process for construction that respects various logistical requirements; select materials; and support the construction phase with oversight and management.

A space architect does all of these things for spacecrafts and habitats in nonterrestrial environments, such as microgravity conditions, interplanetary transit, and lunar and planetary surface locations. The environmental concerns of space architecture are much more challenging than for terrestrial architecture, mainly because we are still trying to understand the conditions and best responses for environments beyond our home planet.

HOW DOES SCIENCE APPLY?

Planning, designing, and overseeing projects intended for use in space allows me to constantly learn new things. While facing the challenges of my work, the basics of science are a very real part of daily life. For instance, every action has an equal and opposite reaction. When my team designs a restraint for the ISS crew to use in space, we have to remember that if a crew member had to push down on the device, that action would send him or her flying across the module! Also, in microgravity or "free fall" there can be no air convection, so hot air does not rise and cold air does not fall. We have to consider what that means for moving air around, especially in places such as the exercise area—even sweat floats in space. During my school days, those scientific principles were always just theoretical ideas I had to memorize; now, I really have to apply those principles every day.

SOLUTIONS FROM NATURE

Working on a component designed for space typically requires solving several different problems at once. Essentially, the resulting product must be very light, usable, simple to install, easy to see, and somehow less time-consuming or expensive than the current state-of-the-art component. Often my approach to solving the various problems is to put the current version out of my mind completely, start at the beginning, and think about what the element really is, what it must do, and how it may have to function. Usually a solution already exists in nature. Nature is a genius at achieving what I call an optimized solution—one that not only solves several problems at once, but does so elegantly and in a reproducible way. Therefore, it often makes sense to study and apply nature's design when creating a modern system or technology [called *biomimetics*].

ADVICE FOR STUDENTS?

A space architect must be fully qualified to practice architecture and, in addition, should have practical

Constance Adams applies scientific principles every day.

experience and special training in engineering or science. Interested students must stay on top of what is happening in science and, specifically, space research. Also, because architects collaborate across many disciplines, the ability to communicate clearly is a fundamental skill. The worlds of engineering, science, and architecture differ widely in issues, values, goals, and terminology.

We are at such an early stage in space research, I imagine myself to be like the masons of the middle ages who laid the foundations and cornerstones

	EDUCATION	ON THE WEB	RELATED CAREERS
BONUS POINTS	BA, social studies; MA, architecture; licensed and registered architect	ISS *(spaceflight.nasa.gov/ station)*	structures engineer, materials scientist, landscape architect, aerospace-model technician, aerodynamicist

of cathedrals. Those people knew that the value of their work would not be seen for generations and that their greatest accomplishments would not matter much in their lifetime. But like them, I do my best and hope that my work will constitute a useful foundation for those who will come after me. With a good start, we may yet learn to live appropriately on Earth and take that knowledge to the exploration of our solar system and beyond. Today's students are our future space explorers, researchers, and architects. [To read about a typical day in this career, visit *www.nsta.org/high school/ connections.aspx.*]

Technology—and Toys

GIS SPECIALIST

In October 2002, in the midst of the terrifying Washington DC sniper attacks, a team of specialists was asked to help search for the suspects. Independent of the official investigation, the team analyzed and mapped attack locations to identify where the snipers were most likely residing. It was challenging and exciting to assist in the search efforts, but dreadful to know that the snipers could strike again at any moment. The team described is the Mapping and Analysis for Public Safety (MAPS) program, led by Ronald Wilson. As a Geographic Information Systems (GIS) specialist, Wilson uses mapping technology and science to understand crime from a geographical perspective.

DESCRIBE THIS FIELD.

From determining the scope of global warming to identifying a city's high-crime areas to navigating trips in cars, GIS is becoming more and more a part of our everyday lives. GIS specialists work to answer location-related questions about society—where things are occurring, where they are not, and where they are changing. The questions may relate to national security, urban planning, transportation analysis, environmental hazards, epidemiology, forest fires, voting patterns, or crime investigation. Finding solutions to the questions requires several steps and always involves geography, the "where" factor.

A specialist trying to learn about a city's crime patterns may gather location data on 911 calls, illegal incidences, and police arrests. Spatial-analysis tools are then used to evaluate the data and create maps that show, in graphic detail, pictures of where these activities occur over time. Using this information, police resources can be deployed effectively to reduce crime.

FIGHTING CRIME.

I manage the MAPS program in the U.S. Department of Justice. Through the application of GIS and the development of new tools [spatial technologies], my team helps state and local law enforcement agencies better visualize spatial crime patterns. For example, we created a spatial statistics software package that can be used to analyze *hot spots*, which are high-crime density areas. By producing analytical maps, the software helps police identify high-crime areas, the types of crime being committed, and the best ways to respond. My team also supports research on geographic aspects of crime. For instance, we analyze demographic and economic data in city neighborhoods to learn about why crimes occur in some areas and not others.

FINDING A NICHE.

While some people understand the world through numbers or stories, I identify with the world geographically. In essence, I see life and relationships as a big map. I have always used spatial reasoning to process information and form ideas. For instance, if a friend asks me for a local restaurant recommendation, I visualize the entire neighborhood—including coffee shops, retail stores, and streets—and make a suggestion based on the "whole picture."

I initially trained to be a police officer [most of my family is in law enforcement], but my innate interest in geography led me to fight crime from behind the scenes instead. To improve my programming skills and create better GIS software, I am taking graduate courses in software engineering. It is rewarding to have an idea, sit down at a computer, and create an innovative tool to solve a specific problem. My next venture is to pursue a doctorate in criminology to round out my education as a specialist in the geographic study of crime.

ADVICE FOR STUDENTS?

Geography is more than just the study of Earth and its features; this unique science looks at interactions among people and the world. Interested students should pursue a college education in geography with a focus on GIS or, alternatively, obtain a professional certificate in GIS. To use GIS effectively, it is vital to understand the key principles of geography such as proximity [closeness], dispersion [movement], and spatial interaction [relationships among people and things]. Also, computer programming is essential to create solution-specific GIS tools.

BONUS POINTS	EDUCATION	ON THE WEB	RELATED CAREERS
	BS, geology; MS, geography; pursuing MS, software engineering	MAPS (www.ojp.usdoj.gov/nij/maps); GIS Day (www.gisday.com)	cartographer, computer programmer, remote sensing analyst, crime analyst, market analyst, urban planner

WHAT WE EAT

What We Eat

NASA FOOD SCIENTIST

For most of us, food is almost always within reach. Food scientists make this possible by using chemistry, engineering, biology, and nutrition to preserve, process, package, and deliver the foods we need. In space, food is not so easy to come by, which is why food scientist Michele Perchonok develops food for astronauts. At NASA's Johnson Space Center (JSC), Perchonok's work has become more challenging as NASA plans and prepares for two-and-a-half to three-year Mars missions. Astronauts on these voyages need not only prepackaged food but also supplies that enable them to prepare real meals, process foods into edible ingredients [turning wheat into wheat flour into bread, for example], and even grow crops.

DESCRIBE THIS CAREER.

In the JSC Space Food Systems Laboratory, food scientists develop products for the Space Shuttle, International Space Station, and Exploration programs. For the Space Shuttle and Space Station, we develop, produce, package, and write specifications for astronaut food products. Fueled by the Vision for Space Exploration, the NASA-wide Exploration program plans for future missions in our solar system, starting with the Moon and followed by voyages to Mars. As part of this preparation, we evaluate new food packaging materials; develop recipes that use only a limited number of crops [soybeans, wheat, peanuts, vegetables, and fruits, for example] and resupply items [examples are dried milk, spices, and cocoa powder]; determine how the acceptance of freeze-dried foods and powdered drinks changes if the foods are rehydrated with hot, ambient, or cold water; and conduct shelf-life testing to determine how long the foods are acceptable and nutritious.

A shelf-life investigation might involve determining if a thermally processed NASA food item has a shelf life of three years. The food is stored at a control temperature of 40°F [about 4°C] and also at 70°F and 95°F [approximately 21°C and 35°C] to determine how variations in temperature may affect the food quality in relation to the control. To minimize data variability, we analyze multiple samples and test the food every four to six months for the three-year duration of the investigation.

WHAT IS A TYPICAL DAY LIKE?

I am involved more with planning and managing projects and investigations rather than conducting experiments in the actual lab. As a project manager, I interact with food scientists and dietitians in the food lab to stay updated on investigations and provide input when needed, coordinate research for external NASA-funded university projects, and collaborate with other JSC engineers and scientists. For example, a JSC team is working on cargo stowage volume for the Crew Exploration Vehicle—our new spacecraft for human space exploration, which should be built and flying by 2014. I provide the team with food stowage volumes, mass, and reasons why our products should be stowed in hard containers instead of soft bags [hard packaging permits less damage and greater integrity]. I also review food-related requirements for the vehicle, such as why we prefer smooth versus pitted surfaces in the galley [smooth surfaces are easier to clean and minimize the possibility of bacterial growth].

ANY ADVICE FOR STUDENTS?

First, a good science background is required—in chemistry, biology, engineering, microbiology, or nutrition, for example. The next step involves understanding how to apply the science to food. Some food scientists may obtain all of their degrees, undergraduate through graduate school, specifically in food science. As a chemistry major in college, I was introduced to food science during a summer internship in the research and development lab at Dunkin' Donuts.

I love that, whatever I do, I can see a direct application. When I worked in the food industry, it was exciting to see products I developed end up on grocery store shelves. Now, at NASA, I help our current and future astronauts. It doesn't hurt that every day when I drive up to JSC, I see rockets on display at the entrance—even after working here for more than five years, the sight still gives me a thrill.

BONUS POINTS	EDUCATION BS, chemistry; MS, food science; PhD, food chemistry, minors in nutritional biochemistry and marketing	ON THE WEB Institute of Food Technologists (www.ift.org)	RELATED CAREERS inspection lab technician, nutritionist, research chef, food and drug lawyer

FOODBORNE DISEASE EPIDEMIOLOGIST

We are often warned about risks of well-known foodborne bacteria, such as salmonella and *E. coli*. But did you know that these infections are just 2 of more than 250 different identified foodborne diseases? The Centers for Disease Control and Prevention (CDC) estimates that 76 million cases of foodborne illness occur in the United States each year. Five thousand are fatal. Most of these illnesses are caused by a variety of bacteria, viruses, and parasites, and the remaining are poisonings triggered by harmful toxins or chemicals. To Jack Guzewich, a foodborne disease epidemiologist with the Food and Drug Administration's (FDA) Center for Food Safety and Applied Nutrition, every outbreak is a new mystery. The mysteries unravel as Guzewich discovers how foods become contaminated and works to prevent similar outbreaks.

WHAT LED YOU TO THIS FIELD?

I had no idea such a career even existed when I was in high school or college. I learned about food epidemiology—the causes, distribution, and control of foodborne disease in populations—after I received formal training in my first job as a sanitarian with the New York State Health Department. I like solving puzzles, and every report of a foodborne illness is a new challenge. Piecing together these puzzles requires knowledge and support from a number of disciplines, including epidemiology, microbiology, chemistry, and environmental health.

DESCRIBE YOUR JOB.

I coordinate the work being done by state and local health departments, the CDC, and FDA field staff to ensure the best possible investigation and a rapid response to foodborne illness outbreaks. A typical day for a field staff food epidemiologist is different from my job. Field staff receive illness and outbreak reports, conduct investigations, and interpret the findings. Investigations can last from a few days to weeks if they are local in nature. If contamination sources come from other states or countries, federal agencies then get involved and investigations can last from weeks to months.

Essentially, investigations involve determining how food was prepared and interviewing

124

people—both healthy and sick—exposed to the suspected food. There is no one syndrome that constitutes foodborne illness—the different diseases have an assortment of symptoms. However, because the microbe or toxin enters the body through the gastrointestinal tract, the first indications of foodborne illness are often nausea, vomiting, abdominal cramps, and diarrhea. A field epidemiologist must know which agents make people sick in order to obtain proper clinical specimens for laboratory tests. Biostatistics are then used to identify which foods are likely culprits in connection with the illness. Based on the findings, actions to prevent future illnesses are carried out.

Programs that maintain foodborne illness statistics include FoodNet—an active, population-based surveillance system of laboratory-diagnosed illnesses in 10 states—and PulseNet, which works at the DNA level. FoodNet quantifies and monitors the incidence of infections caused by enteric pathogens transmitted commonly through food. PulseNet uses pulsed-field gel electrophoresis (PFGE) to distinguish strains of disease-causing agents, such as *E. coli* or salmonella. PFGE produces DNA fingerprints of these agents, which are submitted electronically to a dynamic database for rapid comparison to related cases of illness and contaminated foods.

ANY ADVICE FOR STUDENTS?

A precollege science and math course track provides a good foundation. Students should contact a food epidemiologist at their local health department and question that individual about investigations conducted in the past. Students may even be invited to observe or participate in an investigation, which can be good exposure to this and other interesting public health careers.

The minimum educational background required is a bachelor's degree. As undergraduates, students should major in biological sciences or environmental health and build strong skills in biostatistics. Students should plan to go on for a master's degree, or even a doctorate, in public health with plenty of elective epidemiology courses.

BONUS POINTS	EDUCATION AA, biology lab technology; BS, biology; MPH, environmental health	ON THE WEB Food and Drug Administration Center for Food Safety and Applied Nutrition (*www.cfsan.fda. gov*); Centers for Disease Control and Prevention National Center for Infectious Diseases (*www. cdc.gov/ncidod/diseases/ food/index.htm*)	RELATED CAREERS physician, nurse, sanitarian, microbiologist, laboratory technician, dietitian, veterinarian, food technologist

FOOD TECHNOLOGIST

A longer-lasting, riper tomato is only one example of how recombinant DNA technology—a new combination of DNA molecules that are not found together naturally—has paved new avenues for food science around the world. Chances are you are already eating foods with biotechnology-derived ingredients. A vast array of foods available today are tasty, nutritious, safe, and convenient because of the research and development carried out by people such as Kristen Girard, a principal food scientist in Ocean Spray's Ingredient Technology Group (ITG). Ocean Spray cranberry ingredients can be found in foods from cereals to dairy products and even nutraceuticals [food or dietary supplement ingredients that provide health benefits], due largely to unique processes developed by the company's food technologists.

Food technologists research global trends in the food industry to provide innovative and creative foods that people want to try. They can formulate foods to taste, feel, look, and smell good. By combining culinary traditions with technology innovations, food scientists like Girard create products that are appealing and accepted by consumers.

HOW DO YOU DEVELOP A NEW FOOD?

ITG's goal is to find creative, profitable ways to use cranberries that are not used in trademark fruit juices. We work with large and small food companies to help them incorporate cranberries into their applications. The cranberries could be in the form of concentrate or puree or dried and sweetened [most commonly known as Craisins].

Food technology comes into play when developing a new ingredient, which starts in the lab. When developing an innovative Craisin, for example, ITG has to create an original formula with all the necessary ingredients. Several formulas are experimented with until the desired formula is fine-tuned. Then the processing work begins. At this juncture, we are ready to scale up the formula in the pilot plant. The pilot plant houses the smaller-scale version of the equipment that would be used in a large processing plant. This enables us to test out many processing variables and come up with the optimal product. Once the parameters are set in the pilot plant— processing temperatures, cook times, packaging requirements, and shelf life—it is time to ramp up to large quantities in the production plant. This way we have enough product inventory to offer customers.

DESCRIBE A TYPICAL DAY AT WORK.

If I am not developing a new product or supporting a production run in a processing plant, then I spend my day on technical support for our ingredient sales people. A customer might need help with formulations, a specification, or nutritional information, for example. Much of my time is also spent on the road attending industry trade shows around the world—not only within the United States, but also such countries as England, Italy, Norway, and Denmark—to educate customers about Ocean Spray and our ingredient product line and to help them develop a new finished product utilizing cranberries.

Kristen Girard develops products with Ocean Spray's Ingredient Technology Group.

ADVICE FOR STUDENTS?

Job fairs are a good place to ask questions. For every food company that exists, there are one or several food technologists behind the scenes developing, processing, testing, supporting, and helping to sell the products. Students would benefit by investigating resources on the internet. Schools that offer food science as an undergraduate degree—such as Penn State, Cornell University, Rutgers University, and the University of California at Davis—are also good sources of information. To become a food technologist, a bachelor of science degree is needed.

HOW DID YOU BECOME INVOLVED IN FOOD TECHNOLOGY?

Throughout my childhood, I always had a love for science. Growing up in Fairhope, Alabama, provided plenty of opportunities to explore the beaches, woods, and swamps—we even had alligators and cottonmouth snakes that hung out in our back yard. In high school, I had an inspiring biology and genetics teacher who could make

BONUS POINTS	EDUCATION	ON THE WEB	RELATED CAREERS
	BS, biology and secondary education	Institute of Food Technology (*www.ift.org*)	food microbiologist, food inspector, dietitian

breeding fruit flies or dissecting frogs the most captivating part of my day. That teacher became a mentor, and, because of her, I aspired to become a science teacher. I obtained a bachelor's degree in biology and secondary education and enjoyed teaching for a couple of years until deep budget cuts in state education led me to use my science background in another field. I accepted a job as a food scientist for Ocean Spray Cranberries and have never looked back. This is my 15th year.

What We Eat

PLANT GENETICIST

Gregor Mendel's work with pea plants in the 1800s established theories of heredity and long-standing genetic principles. Scientists have come a long way in understanding the inheritance of traits at the molecular level, gene interaction, and environmental influences. As technology advances, so does the ability to better appreciate genetic diversity. Plant geneticists, such as John Stommel, use traditional research and biotechnology-based approaches to develop plants with improved quality, nutritive value, consumer appeal, disease resistance, stress tolerance, and productivity.

WHAT DOES A PLANT GENETICIST DO?

Most people are aware of the work that scientists around the world are doing to sequence the human genome and its impact on research in the medical community. Similar efforts are underway in major crop plants, enabling us to identify and better use the genes that account for diversity in plant communities.

At the U.S. Department of Agriculture's Vegetable Laboratory, we conduct basic research to help us understand the genetic and physiological basis for a particular trait—such as nutritive value, culinary quality, or disease resistance—and use that knowledge in applied research to develop an improved cultivated plant [cultivar] that benefits farmers and consumers. Basic research may involve using classical genetics and molecular biology. In applied research, we use traditional plant breeding, genetics, and biotechnology-based approaches.

DESCRIBE YOUR CURRENT PROJECTS.

My research program focuses on genetic improvement—primarily in fruit quality and nutritive value—of the tomato, pepper, and eggplant. All three species have many wild relatives, which in turn have a variety of attributes such as fruit color, vitamin content, flavor components, and processing quality. The genetic diversity of the wild relatives presents opportunities not only to improve conventional forms of the species, but also to develop novel forms not available in the market.

For example, the red and orange colors in tomatoes are attributed to the presence of carotenoid pigments that include lycopene and beta-carotene [compounds with well-known health benefits]. We explore wild tomato relatives and natural tomato mutants to identify genes that may enhance levels of these compounds in the cultivated tomato. Similarly, in pepper, we are looking at a different class of pigments with potential human health benefits. In eggplant, we are evaluating phenolic acids, which are potent antioxidants and thus beneficial in the diet.

Using classical genetics, we characterize the inheritance of these traits to better predict the behavior of the gene(s) that influence expression of the trait. Using molecular biology tools, we may identify genetic markers to track these genes in studies and to introduce the genes into adapted cultivars. Likewise, molecular genetic tools are used to characterize the expression of influential genes—that is whether genes are turned on or off in different plants, how the action of one gene may affect the action of others, and how genes from exotic plant sources may function in cultivars.

The work spans research in the laboratory, greenhouse, and field environment. The interdisciplinary nature of the research often requires collaboration with other scientists who are experts in specialized areas of plant physiology, plant pathology, postharvest biology, and human nutrition.

ADVICE FOR STUDENTS?

Today's plant geneticist requires a strong background in plant sciences, genetics, and molecular biology. A familiarity with the developing field of bioinformatics is helpful as well.

Colleges, universities, and state and federal labs commonly support internship programs for aspiring students interested in scientific careers. Internships provide valuable opportunities for high school students to assist with research projects and conduct projects of their own in a laboratory. For students, one-on-one training and interaction with scientists provides new and unique insights into the scientific process.

BONUS POINTS	EDUCATION BS, biology; PhD, Plant Breeding and Plant Genetics	ON THE WEB USDA Agricultural Research Service (www.ars.usda.gov)	RELATED CAREERS geneticist, agricultural engineer, nutritionist, food technologist, botanist, horticulturist, plant buyer

REFERENCES

Aylett, R. 2006. *Robots: Bringing intelligent machines to life.* Hauppauge, NY: Barron's Educational Series.

Brown, D. 2003. *The da Vinci code.* New York: Random House.

Deetz, J. 1996. *In small things forgotten: The archaeology of early American life.* Garden City, NY: Anchor Books.

Franklin, S. 1995. *Artificial minds.* Cambridge, MA: Bradford Books/MIT Press.

Grand, S. 2001. *Creation: Life and how to make it.* Cambridge, MA: Harvard University Press.

Khan, D. 1996. *The codebreakers: The comprehensive history of secret communication from ancient times to the internet.* New York: Scribner's.

Orser, C. 2003. *Historical archaeology.* Upper Saddle River, NJ: Prentice Hall.

Plant Talk. 2007. 100 plant facts: The diversity of the plant kingdom. *www.plant-talk.org/pages/pfacts1.html.*

Schneier, B. 1996. *Applied cryptography.* New York: John Wiley and Sons.

Schneier, B. 2002. *Secrets and lies.* New York: John Wiley and Sons.

Stone, W., B. am Ende, and M. Paulsen. 2002. *Beyond the deep: The deadly descent into the world's most treacherous cave.* New York: Warner Books.

Ubick, D., P. Paquin, P. E. Cushing, and V. Roth. 2005. *Spiders of North America: An identification manual.* Ottawa, Canada: American Arachnological Society.

INDEX

Numbers in *italics* refer to photos.

A

AA (associate of arts)
    biology lab technology, 125
    occupational studies, 83
acoustics of musical instruments, 43
Adams, Constance, 116–118, *117*
Adams, Robert, 62–63, *63*
adaptability, 17
adventure, careers and, 6–12
Aerospace Corporation, 6
Allgood, Greg, 94–95, *95*
Am Ende, Barbara Anne, 6–7, *7*
American Association for Respiratory Care, 64
American Board of Forensic Anthropology, 90, 91
animal nutritionist, 16–18
animal-related careers, 14–33
anthropology, usefulness of, 108, 109
apiculture. *See* honey bee scientist
Applied Cryptography (Schneier), 79
applied sport science, 68
aquaculture veterinarian, 19–21
aquatic conservation biologist, 25–27
Aquavet, 20
arachnologist, 14–15
archaeologist, historical, 84–86
architect
    landscape, 40–41
    space, 116–118
Arizona Fish and Wildlife Research Cooperative, 27
Arrow Dynamics, 112
arson investigations, 82
art conservationist, 38–39
Artificial Minds (Franklin), 115
artificial intelligence expert, 114–115
art-related careers, 36–43
astronauts, 10–12
    food for, 122
astronomical artist, 36–37
astronomy, 108
athletes, working with. *See* sport biomechanist
Attix, Deborah, 73–75, *74*
automotive technician, 110–111

Aveda, 105
Aylett, Ruth, 114–115

B

BA (bachelor of arts)
    anthropology, 91
    anthropology and government, 86
    art/French, 39
    social studies, 117
Baltimore County Police Department Crime Scene Unit, 80
Barger, M. Susan, 38–39
Beauchamp, James, 42–43
bee-string therapy, 23–24
Beyond the Deep (Am Ende), 6
BFA (Bachelor of Fine Arts), 37
biochemistry, 99
    usefulness of, 94
biodiversity
    aquatic conservation biologist and, 25
    arachnologist and, 14
    shark advocate and, 31–33
bioinformatics, 130
biological anthropology, 89, 90
biology, usefulness of, 49, 88, 91, 104, 106, 108, 115, 123
biostatistics, 125
Birchfield, Jason, 80–81, *81*
bomb investigator, 82–83, *83*
bone detective, 89–91
BS (bachelor of science)
    allied health education, 66
    atmospheric science, 53
    biochemistry, 9, 21
    biology, 3, 15, 27, 37, 61, 95, 99, 106, 125, 130
    chemistry, 104, 123
    criminal justice, 81
    ecology and evolutionary biology, 27
    engineering, aerospace, 72
    engineering, electrical, 43
    entomology, 24

environmental Earth science, 47
exercise physiology, 69
geography, 113
geology, 7, 49, 120
geology, environmental, 51
geology/biology, 88
Latin American literature, 56
marine science, 33
molecular biophysics, 21
music, 109
natural resources, 41
nursing, 59
occupational studies, 83
physics, 12, 79, 97
psychology, 75
radiologic science, 63
science writing, 30
zoology, 18
Byrnes, Jeff, 50–51, *51*

C

California, University of, at Davis, 22, 127
The California and Carnegie Planet Search, 36
Cambodia, 26
Carrano, Matthew, 87–88, *88*
CDE (certified diabetes educator), 59
Centers for Disease Control and Prevention (CDC),
    95, 124, 125
certification
    diabetes educator, 59
    emergency medical technician, 9
    forensic anthropologist, 90, 91
    medical dosimetrist, 63
    pulmonary function technologist, 66
    respiratory therapist, 65
Chanel's Research and Development Formulation
    Laboratories, 105, 106
chemist
    cosmetic, 105–106
    green product, 103–104
chemistry, usefulness of, 49, 90, 91, 101, 102, 104,
    106, 123, 124
Chen, Andy, 103–104
Chesapeake Bay Foundation, 28, 30
clinical neuropsychologist, 73–75
CMD (certified medical dosimetrist), 63
coaching, 68

coatings specialist, 96–97
Codebreakers, The (Kahn), 79
Colorado Spider Survey, 14
communications skills, 104, 117
Community Laboratory Research, 52
computer programs, musical, 42
computers, security systems for, 78
computer skills, usefulness of, 37, 43, 51, 88, 111, 115
conservation biologist, aquatic, 25–27
conservation science, art, 39
continuing education for teaching career, 2
Cook, Lynette R., 36–37
Cornell University, 127
cosmetic chemist, 105–106
CPFT (certified pulmonary function technologist), 66
Creation: Life and How to Make It (Grand), 115
Crew Exploration Vehicle, 122
criminal justice, careers related to. *See* bomb
    investigator; forensics services technician; GIS
    specialist
CRT (Certified Respiratory Therapist), 65, 66
cryptographer, 78–79
cryptologist. *See* cryptographer
curator, 15, 87
Cushing, Paula, *14,* 14–15

D

Davis, Wade, 56
deep-cave explorer, 6–7
Deetz, James, 86
Denver Museum of Nature & Science, 14
DeRosa, Brandon, 40–41, *41*
designer
    roller coaster, 112–113
    video game, 108–109
diabetes educator, 58–59
Dierich, Denise, 8–9, *9*
dinosaur paleontologist, 87–88
dissections, human, 90
drinking water project, 95

E

ear, nose, and throat doctor, 70–72
EdD (doctor of education), 63
education level needed
    animal nutritionist, 17

astronaut career, 11
careers in environmental industry, 47
careers in marine science, 29
clinical neuropsychologist, 74
ear, nose, and throat doctor, 71
forensics services technician, 81
paleontologist, 88
radiation therapist, 62–63
respiratory therapist, 65
roller coaster designer, 113
science teaching, 2
Edwards, Mark, 16–18, *17*
Emeagwali, Dale B., 98–99, *99*
emergency medical technician (EMT). *See* paramedic
EMT (emergency medical technician). *See* paramedic
engineering, 106, 113
　　usefulness of, 115, 123
ENT doctors. *See* ear, nose, and throat doctor
entomologist. *See* arachnologist; honey bee scientist
environmental consultant, 46–47
environmental health, 124
environmentally preferred materials, developing,
　　103–104
Environmental Protection Agency (EPA)
　　Green Chemistry Program, 103, 104
epidemiology, 124
ethnobotanist, 54–56
excavations, participation in, 85
exercise science, 69
extension specialists
　　on fish, 19
　　on honey bees, 22–24

F

Facher, Jennifer, 60–61, *61*
Facility Engineering Associates, 46
Fadiman, Maria, 54–56, *55*
Feil, John, 108–109, *109*
fellowship, postdoctoral, 74
fingerprints, 81
firefighter, 8–9
Florida, University of, 19, 72
Food and Drug Administration Center for Food
　　Safety and Applied Nutrition, 124, 125
foodborne disease epidemiologist, 124–125
food epidemiology, 124
FoodNet, 125

food-related careers, 122–130
food science, schools offering, 127
food scientist, NASA, 122–123
food technologist, 126–128
Forde, Evan, 48–49, *49*
Fordham, Sonja, 31–33, *32*
forensic anthropologist, 89–91
forensics services technician, 80–81
France, Diane, 89–91
Franklin, Stan, 115
Fulbright Program, 27
Fuller Ford, 110
Fundamentals of Clinical Neuropsychology (Kolb and
　　Wishaw), 75

G

genetic counselor, 60–61
genetics, 130
geography, usefulness of, 88, 108, 120
geology, usefulness of, 49, 88, 108
Girard, Kristen, 126–128, *127*
GIS specialist, 119–120
Grand, Steve, 115
green product chemist, 103–104
Guild of Natural Science Illustrators (GNSI), 37
Guzewich, Jack, 124–125

H

habitat restoration specialist. *See* landscape architect
Hazardous Device School, 83
health and fitness, careers related to, 58–75
Health Sciences Institute, 95
hearing, theory of, 43
high-crime density areas, analysis of, 119
Hiser, John D., 64–66, *65, 66*
historical archaeologist, 84–86
Historical Archaeology (Orser), 85
Hogan, Zeb, 25–27, *26*
honey, 23
honey bee scientist, 22–24
Howard, Scott, 70–72, *71*
Huautla Expedition (1994), 6, 7
human anatomy, 90
hurricane researcher, 52–53

I

Idaho, University of, 84
Illinois, University of, 42
illustrator, scientific, 36–37
industrial toxicologist, 94–95
In Small Things Forgotten (Deetz), 86
International Association of Astronomical Artists, 37
International Association of Bomb Technicians and
        Investigators, 82
International Flavors and Fragrances, Inc., 100
International Space Station
    architecture and, 116–118
    food for, 122
International Union for Conservation of Nature
        and Natural Resources (IUCN) Red List of
        Threatened Species, 25, 27
internships, 26, 52, 69, 106, 123, 130
    with museums and zoos, 15
    Smithsonian Institution's National Museum of
        Natural History, 14
    Smithsonian Institution's National Zoo, 16
interviews, informational, 106
investigating, careers related to, 79–91

J

job fairs, 127
job market for diabetes educators, 59
Johnson Space Center, 122
JSC Space Food Systems Laboratory, 122

K

Kahn, David, 79

L

landscape architect, 40–41
Landsea, Christopher, 52–53
Laudamiel, Christopher, 100–102, *101*
learning about careers. *See also* internships; volunteer
        positions
    excavations, participation in, 85
    fire departments, ride-along with, 9
    interviews, informational, 106
    job fairs, 127
    mentors, 21
    oceanographic research facility tour, 49

    shadowing, 74
Lewbart, Greg, 21
linguistics, usefulness of, 115
Los Angeles County Arson Explosives Detail, 82
LucasArts, 108

M

MA (master of arts)
    anthropology, 91
    architecture, 117
MAA (master of applied anthropology), 86
Magnavox Company, 42
Mapping and Analysis for Public Safety (MAPS), 119
Marks, Frank, 52
mathematics, usefulness of, 43, 79, 88, 104, 106, 108,
        110, 111, 113, 125
The Matrix, 6
MBA, 59
MD, 72
MEd (master of education), 66
Megafishes (National Geographic), 25
mentors, 21
meteorologist, 52–53
MFA (Master of Fine Arts), 37
Miami Indians, 85
microbial physiology, 99
microbiologist, 98–99
microbiology, usefulness of, 94, 123, 124
molecular biology, 99, 130
Mongolia, 26
Mora, Arcadio, 110–111, *111*
Morgan State University, 98
MPH (master of public health), 95
    environmental health, 125
    health policy and administration, 63
MS (master of science)
    atmospheric science, 53
    chemistry, 102
    computer science, 79
    electrical engineering, 12, 43
    entomology, 24
    environmental science, 3, 30
    exercise physiology, 69
    food science, 123
    genetic counseling, 61
    geography, 120
    geology, 7

landscape architecture, 41
Latin American studies, 56
marine geology/geophysics, 49
public health, 95
zoology, 15
MTV House of Style Video, 106
music, electronic, 42
musical acoustics scientist, 42–43
Mussen, Eric, 22–24, *23*

N

NASA food scientist, 122–123
National Geographic Society, 25, 26
National Oceanic and Atmospheric Administration
    (NOAA), 48, 49
    Atlantic Oceanographic and Meteorological
      Laboratory (AOML), 52
National Science Foundation, 42
National Speleological Society (NSS), 6, 7
National Technical Association, 98
NecroSearch International, 90, 91
Neuropsychological Assessment (Lezak), 75
neuroscience, usefulness of, 115
Nike, 103
nutrition, usefulness of, 94, 123
nutritionist, animal, 16–18

O

oceanographer, 48–49
Ocean Spray's Ingredient Technology Group, 126
Ochoa, Ellen, 10–12, *11*
Oprah Winfrey Show, 94
Orser, Charles, 85
otolaryngologist. *See* ear, nose, and throat doctor
oyster wrangler, 28–30

P

Paleobiology Database, 87
paleontologist, dinosaur, 87–88
paramedic, 8–9
Parrish, Jack, 52
pathology, 94
Penn State, 127
Pennsylvania, University of, 71
people, working with, 61

Perchonok, Michele, 122–123
perfumer, 100–102
PhD (doctor of philosophy)
    animal science, 18
    anthropology, 86
    atmospheric science, 53
    biological anthropology, 91
    chemistry, 104
    clinical psychology, 75
    ecology, 27
    electrical engineering, 12, 43
    engineering physics and materials science, 97
    entomology, 24
    exercise physiology, 69
    food chemistry, 123
    geography, 56
    geology, 7, 51
    materials science/chemistry/history
      of technology, 39
    microbiology, 99
    organismal biology and anatomy, 88
    plant breeding and plant genetics, 130
    toxicology, 95
    zoology, 15
philosophy, usefulness of, 115
physical acoustics, 42–43
physical vapor deposition, 96
physics, usefulness of, 43, 49, 90, 91, 104, 106, 108,
    110, 113, 115
physiology, 94
Pittsburgh, University of, 61
plant geneticist, 129–130
plant resources, sustainability of. *See* ethnobotanist
plant sciences, 130
Plant Talk, 54
Plotkin, Mark, 56
pollen, 23
Polyglot Paleontologist, The, 87
polysomnography, 64
problem-solving skills
    aquatic veterinarian, 21
    firefighting, 9
Procter & Gamble, 94
propolis, 23
psychology, usefulness of, 109, 115
psychometrician, 74
public speaking skills, 33, 51
PulseNet, 125

R

radiation therapist, 62–63
research and development, 94–106
respiratory therapist, 64–66
restoration of natural sites. *See* landscape architect
Reynolds, Stephanie, 28–30, *29*
Rice, Donna, 58–59
robots, 114
Robots: Bringing Intelligent Machines to Life (Aylett), 114
roller coaster designer, 112–113
Roskoski, Maureen, 46–47, *47*
Rossing, Thomas, 42
royal jelly, 23
RRT (Registered Respiratory Therapist), 65, 66
RT (registered radiation therapist), 63
Rutgers University, 127

S

Salford, University of (U.K.), 114
San Diego Zoo, 17
Sands, Bill, 67–69, *68*
Schneier, Bruce, 78–79
Science of Sound, The (Rossing), 42
science teacher, 2–3
scientific inquiry, understanding of, 90
Secrets and Lies (Schneier), 79
Seko, Kent, 112–113, *113*
shadowing, 74
shark advocate, 31–33
Shark Alliance, 31
Shark Conservation Program at the Ocean
        Conservancy, 31
Smithsonian Institution
    Global Volcanism Program, 51
    National Museum of Natural History, 14, 87
    National Zoo, 16
sociology, usefulness of, 108, 109
space, careers related to
    astronaut, 10–12
    astronomy illustrator, 36–37
    NASA food scientist, 122–123
    planetary volcanologist, 50
    space architect, 116–118
space architect, 116–118
spatial technologies, 119
Spiders of North America: An Identification Manual
        (Ubick, Paquin, Cushing, and Roth), 14

sport biomechanist, 67–69
sports, usefulness of, 68
sport science, 69
statistics, usefulness of, 88
    biostatistics, 125
Stommel, John, 129–130
submersible dives, 49
Sullivan, Patrick, 96–97, *97*

T

teacher, science, 2–3
technology, 108–120
toxicologist, food, 94
toxicologist, industrial, 94–106
toxicology, mechanistic, 94
trade shows, 127
training
    for firefighting, 8
    for NASA flight, 10–11
traveling, 106

U

The UnderseaWorld of Jacques Cousteau (television show),
        48
United Nations Convention on Migratory Species, 27
USA Gymnastics, 68
U.S. Department of Agriculture
    honey bee laboratories, 22
    Vegetable Laboratory, 129
U.S. Olympic Committee (USOC), 68
U.S. Olympic Training Center, 67
Utah, University of, 112

V

Vacuum Arc, 96–97
Vapor Technologies, 96
veterinarian, aquatic, 19–21
video game level designer, 108–109
Villa, Barney T., 82–83, *83*
virology, 99
Vision for Space Exploration, 122
VMD (Veterinariae Medicinae Doctoris), 21
volcanologist, planetary, 50–51
volunteer positions, 3, 15, 52, 54, 61, 71, 88

W

Walter Reed Army Medical Center, 70

Warner, Mark, 84–86, *85*

websites

Acoustical Society of America, 43

American Academy of Forensic Sciences, 81

American Academy of Otolaryngology–Head and Neck Surgery, 72

American Apparel and Footwear Association RSL, 104

American Arachnological Society, 15

American Association for Artificial Intelligence, 115

American Association for Respiratory Care, 65

American Association of Diabetes Educators, 59

American Board of Forensic Anthropology, 91

American Diabetes Association, 59

American Fisheries Society, 21

American Institute for Conservation of Historic and Artistic Works, 39

American Physical Society, 97

American Psychological Association's Division of Clinical Neuropsychology, 75

American Registry of Radiologic Technologists, 63

American Society for Microbiology, 99

American Society of Landscape Architects, 41

American Society of Radiologic Technologists, 63

American Tarantula Society, 15

American Zoo and Aquarium Association, 18

An Introduction to Ethnobotany, 56

Automotive Student Service Educational Training, 111

Beauchamp, James, web page, 43

Bose-Einstein Condensation, 97

Carrano, 88

Centers for Disease Control and Prevention, 95

Centers for Disease Control and Prevention National Center for Infectious Diseases, 125

Chesapeake Bay Foundation, 30

Dinosauria Online, 88

Environmental Careers Organization, 47

EPA's Green Chemistry Program, 104

Eric Mussen, 24

Exploratorium's Sport Science Exhibit, 69

Food and Drug Administration Center for Food Safety and Applied Nutrition, 125

Ford Accelerated Credential Training, 111

GIS Day, 120

Guild of Natural Science Illustrators, 37

Health Sciences Institute, 95

Institute of Food Technologists, 123, 127

International Association for Aquatic Animal Medicine, 21

International Association for Cryptologic Research, 79

International Association for Identification, 81

International Association of Amusement Parks and Attractions, 113

International Association of Astronomical Artists, 37

International Association of Fire Fighters, 9

International Fragrance Association, 102

International Game Developers Association, 109

International Society of Arachnology, 15

International Union for Conservation of Nature and Natural Resources (UICN) Red List of Threatened Species, 27

ISS, 117

Joint Review Committee for Radiologic Technology, 63

Law Enforcement Exploring, 83

MAPS, 120

NASA Astronaut Selection, 12

NASA Johnson Space Center astronaut profiles and experiences, 12

National Association of Emergency Medical Technicians, 9

National Board for Respiratory Care, 65

National Honey Board, 24

National Oceanic and Atmospheric Administration, 49

National Oceanic and Atmospheric Administration/Atlantic Oceanographic and Meteorological Laboratory, 53

National Science Teachers Association, 3

National Security Agency, 79

National Society of Generic Counselors, 61

National Speleological Society, 7

NecroSearch, 91

Ocean Conservancy, 33

RoboCup, 115

Sense of Smell Institute, 102

Shark Alliance, 33

Smithsonian Institution's Global Volcanism Program, 51

Society for Conservation Biology, 27
Society for Economic Botany, 56
Society for Historical Archaeology, 86
Society of Cosmetic Chemists, 106
Society of Toxicology, 95
University of North Dakota's Volcano World, 51
USDA Agricultural Research Service, 130
U.S. Olympic Internship Program, 69
World Health Organization, 95
Zoological Society of San Diego, 18
West Point, 71
Wilson, Ronald, 119–120
writing skills, usefulness of, 32–33, 49, 51, 53, 99
Wyatt, Amy, 105–106

Y

Yanong, Roy P. E., 19–21, *20*
Youth and Explosives (video), 83

Z

Zito, Mike, 2–3, *3*
Zoological Society of San Diego, 16